CUET

(UG) & Integrated PG

2022

Geography

DU | BHU | JNU | JMI | TISS & etc.

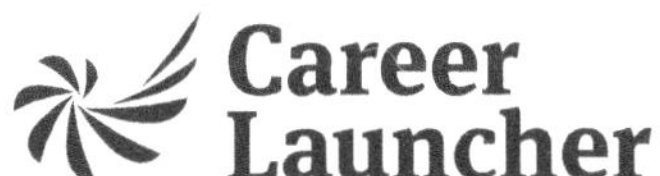

Title   : CUET 2022 : Geography

Language   : English

Editor's Name   : Pravin Choubey, Aparna Aman

Copyright ©   : 2022 CLIP

Typeset & Published by :

Career Launcher Infrastructure (P) Ltd.

A-45, Mohan Cooperative Industrial Area, Near Mohan Estate Metro Station, New Delhi - 110044

Marketed by :

G.K. Publications (P) Ltd.

Plot No. 9A, Sector-27A, Mathura Road, Faridabad, Haryana-121003

ISBN   : **978-93-95101-25-7**

For product information :

Visit ***www.gkpublications.com*** or email to ***gkp@gkpublications.com***

CONTENTS

GEOGRAPHY

About CUET

A year ago, it would have been unimaginable that cut-offs in Delhi University would skyrocket to 100% for some of the undergraduate courses! While DU has always been known for its high cut-offs, there are several other universities where the story is no different.

However, the National Education Policy 2020 (NEP) aims to do away with the tyranny of the ever-rising cut-offs by introducing a Common Entrance Test for all the Central Universities in the country. NEP not only proposes a holistic approach in evaluating the students by giving them the option to select subjects based on their interest, but it also aims to simplify the process of admission to higher-education institutes.

To start with, there would be a Common Entrance Test for all the Central Universities, which would be conducted twice a year from 2022. While this might sound like a new concept to many, the fact is, there is already a CUET, which is conducted for the Central Universities established in or after 2009. As many as 14 of them already admit students based on their performance in the entrance test. The CUET scores are also accepted by four state universities of the country.

The proposed CUET aims to assess conceptual understanding and application of knowledge; and also, to lessen the burden of appearing in multiple tests.

CUET Eligibility

Getting into a premier University is every student's dream. The brand value of the University not only facilitates securing a seat in a master's program in a national/international institute, but also helps in getting job offers through campus placements.

Entry to a Central University, in most cases earlier, was based on merit, i.e., marks secured in Class XII Board exams. However, from the academic year 2021, all Central Universities will also consider the CUET score for admissions into their Undergraduate programs.

CUET 2022: Eligibility Criteria

While the official criteria will be learnt once the CUET 2021 notification is released, the stipulations are not expected to change much from those of previous years.

- A candidate must have passed Class XII (10+2) or equivalent from a recognized education Board.

- If the respective Board awards grades (or CGPA), the conversion factor given by the Board must be used to compute the percentage of marks.

- Candidates, who have completed their Class XII in 2021, and have passed the Board exams, will also be eligible to apply for CUET 2022.

Eligibility: Class XII Students

While CUET is for students who have passed the Class XII (or equivalent) Board exams, any student who is appearing for the Class XII Board exam in 2022 is also eligible to apply for CUET 2021. The candidate would be required to produce the marksheets and relevant certificates as mandated by the participating Central University, and follow the timelines provided for admissions.

Key Points

- Each participating Central University is free to decide its own eligibility criteria for admissions.

- The weightages for CUET and Class XII Board exam results(if, applicable) will be at the sole discretion of the Central University, to which admission is being sought.

- As of date, CUET does not have an age limit. However, Central Universities can fix minimum & maximum age limit for admissions to all (or any) of the programs on offer.

Reservation of Seats

As CUET is an entrance exam for admissions to Undergraduate courses at the Central Universities, which have been established under an Act of the Parliament, each Central University must follow the norms set by the Government of India, with respect to intake and reservation of seats.

Generally, the following break-up is followed:

Category	Reservation
Scheduled Castes	15%
Scheduled Tribes	7.5%
Other Backward Classes (Non-Creamy)	27%
Persons with Disability	5%

Some institutions might even have provisions for the Economically Weaker Sections, which can account for 10% of the total seats. These EWS seats are carved out from the Open Category.

To avail of the reservation benefit based on caste (or any other category as specified), a candidate must be able to produce valid documents/certificates to support such claims.

Conclusion

It is essential for every candidate to check the validity of their candidature for CUET, as well as the Central University he/she is applying to. The candidate should be aware of the documents that might be required while applying for the exam, or during the admissions.

CUET 2022 notification is expected in March 2022, and registration is also going to start then.

CUET: Exam Pattern

Examination Structure for CUET (UG) -2022:

CUET (UG) –2022 will consist of the following 4 Sections:

    Section IA –13 Languages
    Section IB –19 Languages
    Section II –27 Domain specific Subjects
    Section III –General Test

Choosing options from each Section is not mandatory. Choices should match the requirements of the desired University.

Broad features of CUET (UG) -2022 are as follows:

Section	Subjects/ Tests	Questions to be Attempted	Question Type	Duration
Section IA – Languages	There are 13* different languages. Any of these languages may be chosen.	40 questions to be attempted out of 50 in each language	Language to be tested through Reading Comprehension (based on different types of passages–Factual, Literary and Narrative, [Literary Aptitude and Vocabulary]	45 Minutes for each language
Section IB – Languages	There are 19** Languages. Any other language apart from those offered in Section I A may be chosen.			
Section II - Domain	There are 27*** Domains specific subjects being offered under this Section. A candidate may choose a maximum of Six (06) Domains as desired by the applicable University/Universities.	40 Questions to be attempted out of 50	• Input text can be used for MCQ Based Questions • MCQs based on NCERT Class XII syllabus only	
Section III- General Test	For any such undergraduate programme/ programmes being offered by Universities where a General Test is being used for admission.	60 Questions to be attempted out of 75	• Input text can be used for MCQ Based Questions • General Knowledge, Current Affairs, General Mental Ability, Numerical Ability, Quantitative Reasoning (Simple application of basic mathematical concepts arithmetic/algebra geometry/mensuration/s tat taught till Grade 8), Logical and Analytical Reasoning	

*** Languages (13):** Tamil, Telugu, Kannada, Malayalam, Marathi, Gujarati, Odiya, Bengali, Assamese, Punjabi, English, Hindi and Urdu

**** Languages (19):** *French, Spanish, German, Nepali, Persian, Italian, Arabic, Sindhi, Kashmiri, Konkani, Bodo, Dogri, Maithili, Manipuri, Santhali, Tibetan, Japanese, Russian, Chinese.*

***** Domain Specific Subjects (27):** 1. Accountancy/ Book Keeping 2. Biology/ Biological Studies/ Biotechnology/Biochemistry 3. Business Studies 4. Chemistry 5. Computer Science/ Informatics Practices 6. Economics/ Business Economics 7. Engineering Graphics 8.Entrepreneurship 9. Geography/Geology 10. History 11. Home Science 12.Knowledge Tradition and Practices of India 13. Legal Studies 14. Environmental Science 15. Mathematics 16. Physical Education/ NCC /Yoga 17.Physics 18.Political Science 19. Psychology 20. Sociology 21. Teaching Aptitude 22. Agriculture 23. Mass Media/ Mass Communication 24. Anthropology 25. Fine Arts/Visual Arts (Sculpture/ Painting)/Commercial Arts, 26. Performing Arts – (i) Dance (Kathak/ Bharatnatyam/Oddisi/ Kathakali/Kuchipudi/ Manipuri (ii) Drama- Theatre (iii) Music General (Hindustani/ Carnatic/ RabindraSangeet/ Percussion/ Non-Percussion), 27. Sanskrit *[For all Shastri (Shastri 3 years/ 4 years Honours) Equivalent to B.A./B.A. Honours courses i.e. Shastri in Veda, Paurohitya (Karmakand), Dharamshastra, Prachin Vyakarana, Navya Vyakarana, Phalit Jyotish, Siddhant Jyotish, Vastushastra, Sahitya,Puranetihas, Prakrit Bhasha,Prachin Nyaya Vaisheshik, Sankhya Yoga, Jain Darshan, Mimansa, AdvaitaVedanta, Vishihstadvaita Vedanta, Sarva Darshan, a candidate may choose Sanskrit as the Domain].*

- A Candidate can choose a maximum of **any 3 languages** from Section IA and Section IB taken together. (One of the languages chosen needs to be in lieu of Domain specific subjects)
- Section II offers 27 Subjects, out of which a candidate may choose a **maximum of 6 Subjects.**
- Section III comprises **General Test.**
- For choosing Languages (upto 3) from Section IA and IB and a maximum of 6 Subjects from Section II and General Test under Section III, the Candidate must refer to the requirements of his/her intended University.

Mode of the Test	Computer Based Test-CBT
Test Pattern	Objective type with Multiple Choice Questions
Medium	13 languages (*Tamil, Telugu, Kannada, Malayalam, Marathi, Gujarati, Odiya, Bengali, Assamese, Punjabi, English, Hindi and Urdu)*
Syllabus	**Section IA & IB:** Language to be tested through Reading Comprehension (based on different types of passages–Factual, Literary and Narrative [Literary Aptitude & Vocabulary]
	Section II : As per NCERT model syllabus as applicable to Class XII only
	Section III : General Knowledge, Current Affairs, General Mental Ability, Numerical Ability, Quantitative Reasoning (Simple application of basic mathematical concepts arithmetic/algebra geometry/mensuration/stat taught till Grade 8), Logical and Analytical Reasoning

Level of questions for CUET (UG) -2022:

All questions in various testing areas will be benchmarked at the level of Class XII only. Students having studied Class XII Board syllabus would be able to do well in CUET (UG) – 2022.

Number of attempts:

If any University permits students of previous years of class XII to take admission in the current year also, such students would also be eligible to appear in CUET (UG) – 2022.

Choice of Languages and Subjects:

Generally the languages/subjects chosen should be the ones that a student has opted in his latest Class XII Board examination. However, if any University permits any flexibility in this regards, the same can be exercised under CUET (UG) -2022 also. Candidates must carefully refer to the eligibility requirements of various Central Universities in this regard. Moreover, if the subject to be studied in the Undergraduate course is not available in the list of **27 Domain Specific Subject** being offered, the Candidate may choose the Subject closest to his choice for e.g. For Biochemistry the candidate may choose Biology.

Candidates are advised to visit the NTA CUET (UG)-2022 official website **https://cuet.samarth.ac.in/** for latest updates regarding the Examination.

CUET Syllabus

CUET Syllabus

Before you start your preparation for any entrance exam, it is important to understand the syllabus. Otherwise, your prep will be directionless, and you might be left wondering where things might have gone wrong!

With more than 1.68 lakh seats on offer for the undergraduate courses at the 54 Central Universities, CUET is one the most competitive examinations. For this very reason, while preparing for the exam, you will need to adopt a structured approach. And in doing that, understanding the syllabus is a critical step.

CUET 2022 Overview

CUET 2022 will be a Computer-Based Test (CBT), commonly referred to as an online exam. However, there is a difference between the two terms: CBT and online. In CBT, the questions are kept constant and simply presented in an online format; whereas in an Online Test, questions are stored as a bank, and the system decides which questions are to be presented to the candidate, based on a pre-defined logic.

CUET 2022 is likely to be a General Ability Test, with focus on English Language, Numerical Ability, Logical & Analytical Reasoning, along with General Awareness and Current Affairs.

CUET 2022 Syllabus

The CUET 2022 exam pattern gives a good idea about what is in store for the candidate and how one needs to prepare for the exam.

- **English Language:** The questions in this section will test one's proficiency in the language, based on comprehension passages, fundamentals of grammar, and vocabulary. In the Comprehension section, candidates will be evaluated on their understanding of a passage and its central theme, meanings of words used therein, etc. The Grammar section entails correcting grammatically incorrect sentences, filling of blanks in sentences with appropriate words, etc. Questions on synonyms & antonyms will check one's command over English vocabulary.
- **Numerical Ability:** Questions on Numerical Ability will test the candidate's knowledge of elementary mathematics. Areas like arithmetic, number system, basics of algebra, and modern maths will be central to these types of questions.
- **Logical & Analytical Reasoning:** This section tests the candidate's ability to identify patterns & logical links, and rectify illogical arguments. It can include a variety of Logical Reasoning questions, such as those on syllogisms, logical sequences, analogies, etc., along with Analytical Reasoning questions on series, directions, clocks & calendars, arrangements, and puzzles to name a few.
- **General Awareness and Current Affairs:** The General Awareness section includes static general knowledge, while questions on Current Affairs will gauge a candidate's knowledge of national & international current affairs.

CUET 2022 may or may not have a section on subject knowledge. Once the exam notification is out in March, there will be more clarity on this matter.

While there is no syllabus explicitly mentioned by CUET, the broad idea is always presented. One must look at the previous years' papers and solve the sample papers available to form a basic understanding.

About University of Delhi

University of Delhi (commonly known as DU) was established in 1922 and is one of the largest Universities in the country. With 16 faculties, 86 academic departments, 90 colleges and 540 programs on offer, Delhi University is no doubt one of the sought-after University in the country.

With 1, 96,000 students enrolled in UG programs, Delhi University is a valued university and constantly ranked among the top in the country. DU bagged 11th Rank in NIRF 2020 and ranked 6th in QS India Rankings 2020. The University has two Campuses: North and South.

DU UG Programs

Delhi University offers several programs at the undergraduate level. With more than 60 constituent colleges, the Delhi University offers many undergraduate courses.

Please refer to the table below for the important undergraduate courses offered by the DU and the intake across each program.

Program	Intake
B. A (Pass)	11249
B. A (Hons) Geography	788
B. A (Hons) Economics	2754
B. A (Hons) History	2791
B. A (Hons) Political Science	3657
B. A (Hons) Sociology	596
B. A (Hons) Psychology	670
B. A (Hons) Applied Psychology	252
B. A (Hons) Social Work	133
B. A (Hons) Philosophy	783
B. A (Hons) English	2886
B. A (Hons) Hindi	2829
B. A (Hons) Sanskrit	1407
B. A (Hons) Punjabi	214
B. A (Hons) Urdu	207
BA(Hons) French	49

Program	Intake
BA(Hons) German	49
BA(Hons) Spanish	49
BA(Hons) Italian	49
B. Com (Hons)	7953
B.Com (Pass)	7854
Program	Intake
B.Sc. (H) Biomedical Science	162
B.Sc. (H) Botany	937
B.Sc. (H) Chemistry	1487
B.Sc. (H) Computer Science	1265
B.Sc. (H) Electronics	624
B.Sc. (H) Mathematics	2428
B.Sc. (H) Physics	1659
B.Sc. (H) Zoology	944
B.Sc. Life Sciences	1515
B.Sc. Physical Science with Chemistry	703
B.Sc. Physical Science with Computer Science	553
B.Sc. Physical Science with Electronics	247
B. Sc (Hons.) Statistics	476
B. Sc. (Prog.) Applied Physical Science Industrial Chemistry	96
B.Sc. (Hons.) Home Science	900
B. Sc. (Hons.) Psychology	57
B.Sc. (H) Food Technology	179
B.Sc. (H)Instrumentation	99
B.Sc. (H) Microbiology	238
B.Sc. (H) Polymer Science	59
B.SC. Mathematical Science	224
B.SC. (Hons.) Biochemistry	146
B.SC. Industrial Chemistry	78
B.Sc. (Prog.) Physical Science	940
B.SC. (Hons.) Geology	98

DU UG Programs Eligibility:

As the University offers multiple programs and separate intake for male and female candidates, it is important to check the university official website regularly to keep oneself updated about the eligibility for each program, which can change.

DU UG Admissions:

Until 2021, Delhi University admitted students on the basis of class XII marks. From the academic year 2022, admissions to UG programs offered Delhi University will be based on CUET. CUET will be a common entrance for admissions to UG programs offered by all the Central Universities in the country.

Delhi University UG Programs Reservation:

DU being a Central University offers reservations in admissions according to central government rules.

Schedule Caste (SC): 15% of the total seats are reserved for students who belong to SC category.

Schedule Tribe (ST): 7.5% of the total seats are reserved for students belonging to ST Category.

Other Backward Classes (OBC): 27% of the total intake is reserved for students from Other Backward Classes (OBC), excluding those from creamy layer.

Economically Weaker Section (EWS): The University has reserved 10% seats for EWS category, in accordance with the directive of Ministry of Education.

Persons with Disability (PWD): 5% of the seats are reserved on horizontal basis for students from PWD category.

About BHU

Banaras Hindu University (BHU), situated in the holy city of Varanasi, was founded by Pandit Madan Mohan Malviya in cooperation with Dr. Annie Besant, in 1916 under the act of Parliament-B.H.U Act, 1915. BHU, which is a Central University, comprises of 6 Institutes, 14 Faculties, 144 academic departments, and 4 Inter-disciplinary centers, spread over 1300 acres. The University consists of 15,000 students, 1700 teachers and 8000 non-teaching staff.

BHU was ranked 3rd among the Universities in India in 2020. According to university submissions for NIRF 2021, BHU has 10, 585 students pursuing UG programs, of which 236 students are foreign nationals.

BHU UG Programs

BHU offers a host of undergraduate programs including medical and engineering. Through its various faculties, BHU offers a range of programs which caters to students learning abilities. The University along with its main campus, also offers the undergraduate courses from the following colleges: Mahila Mahavidyalaya (MMV); Arya Mahila Post Graduate College (AMPGC), Vasant Kanya Mahavidyalaya (VKM); Vasanta College for Women (VCW); DAV Post Graduate College (DAVPGC) and Rajiv Gandhi South Campus (RGSC).

Please refer to the table below for the important undergraduate courses offered by BHU and the intake across each program/campuses.

Faculty of Arts				
Course	Campus	Intake	Status	Duration
B.A (Hons) Arts	Faculty of Arts	765	Co-Ed	3 Years
	Mahila Mahavidyalaya	286	Women	3 Years
	Arya Mahila Post Graduate College	383	Women	3 Years
	Vasant Kanya Mahavidyalaya	286	Women	3 Years
	Vasanta College for Women	412	Women	3 Years
	DAV Post Graduate College	309	Co-Ed	3 Years
Faculty of Social Sciences				
Course	Campus	Intake	Status	Duration
B.A (Hons) Social Sciences [incl. B. A (Hons) Economics]	Faculty of Social Sciences	573	Co-Ed	3 Years
	Mahila Mahavidyalaya	193	Women	3 Years
	Arya Mahila Post Graduate College	383	Women	3 Years
	Vasant Kanya Mahavidyalaya	249	Women	3 Years
	Vasanta College for Women	210	Women	3 Years
	DAV Post Graduate College	326	Co-Ed	3 Years

Faculty of Commerce				
Course	Campus	Intake	Status	Duration
B. Com (Hons)	Faculty of Commerce	286	Co-Ed	3 Years
	Vasant Kanya Mahavidyalaya	96	Women	3 Years
	Arya Mahila Post Graduate College	96	Women	3 Years
	DAV Post Graduate College	227	Co-Ed	3 Years
	Rajiv Gandhi South Campus, Mirzapur	114	Co-Ed	3 Years
B. Com (Hons) Financial Markets Management	Faculty of Commerce	62	Co-Ed	3 Years
	Rajiv Gandhi South Campus, Mirzapur	62	Co-Ed	3 Years

Institute of Science				
Course	Campus	Intake	Status	Duration
B.Sc (Hons) Maths Group	Faculty of Science	573	Co-Ed	3 Years
	Mahila Mahavidyalaya	96	Women	3 Years
B.Sc (Hons) Bio Group	Faculty of Science	383	Co-Ed	3 Years
	Mahila Mahavidyalaya	193	Women	3 Years

Faculty of Visual Arts				
Course	Campus	Intake	Status	Duration
B.F.A (Bachelor of Fine Arts)	Faculty of Visual Arts	96	Co-Ed	4 Years
Faculty of Arts				
Bachelor of Vocation (Retail and Logistics Management)	Rajiv Gandhi South Campus	62	Co-Ed	3 Years
Bachelor of Vocation (Hospitality & Tourism Management)	Rajiv Gandhi South Campus	62	Co-Ed	3 Years
Bachelor of Vocation (Fashion Designing and Event Management)	Rajiv Gandhi South Campus	62	Co-Ed	3 Years
Bachelor of Vocation (Modern Office Management)	Rajiv Gandhi South Campus	62	Co-Ed	3 Years
Bachelor of Vocation (Food Processing & Management)	Rajiv Gandhi South Campus	62	Co-Ed	3 Years
Bachelor of Vocation (Medical Lab. & Technology)	Rajiv Gandhi South Campus	62	Co-Ed	3 Years

BHU UG Programs Eligibility:

Each of the courses have different eligibility for admissions. To be eligible for admissions, one must fulfil all the criteria as laid down by the respective faculties of the University.

B.A (Hons) Arts/ B.A (Hons) Social Sciences: Candidate must not be more than 22 years of age and must have passed class XII or equivalent with minimum 50% marks in aggregate.

B.A (Hons) Economics: Candidate must not be more than 22 years of age and must have passed class XII or equivalent with minimum 50% marks in aggregate along with mathematics as one of the papers.

B. Com (Hons)/B. Com (Hons) Financial Markets Management: Candidate must not be more than 22 years of age and must have passed class XII or equivalent with minimum 50% marks in aggregate with Commerce/ Economics/Maths/Computer Science/Finance/Financial Markets Management as one of the subjects.

B. Sc (Hons) Maths Group: Candidate must not be more than 22 years of age and must have passed class XII or equivalent with minimum 50% marks in aggregate in the subjects Physics, Maths plus any one of the following: Chemistry, Statistics, Geology, Computer Science, Information Technology and Geography and must have passed in each of the concerned three subjects.

B. Sc (Hons) Bio Group: Candidate must not be more than 22 years of age and must have passed class XII or equivalent with minimum 50% marks in aggregate in the subjects Physics, Chemistry plus any one of the following: Biology, Geology and Geography and must have passed in each of the concerned three subjects.

B. F. A (Bachelor of Fine Arts): Candidate must not be more than 22 years of age and must have passed class XII or equivalent with minimum 50% marks in aggregate.

Bachelor of Vocation: Candidate must have passed class XII or equivalent in any stream (Science for Food Processing and Medical Lab Technology) or level 4 NSQF certificate.

BHU UG Admissions:

Until 2021, admissions to BHU UG courses were based on Undergraduate Entrance Test (UET) conducted by the University. From the academic year 2022, admissions to UG programs offered by BHU will be based on CUET, which will replace the UET. CUET will be a common entrance for admissions to UG programs offered by all the Central Universities in the country.

BHU UG Programs Reservation:

BHU being a Central University offers reservations in admissions according to central government rules.

Schedule Caste (SC): 15% of the total seats are reserved for students who belong to SC category.

Schedule Tribe (ST): 7.5% of the total seats are reserved for students belonging to ST Category.

Other Backward Classes (OBC): 27% of the total intake is reserved for students from Other Backward Classes (OBC), excluding those from creamy layer.

Economically Weaker Section (EWS): The University has reserved 10% seats for EWS category, in accordance with the directive of Ministry of Education.

Persons with Disability (PWD): 5% of the seats are reserved on horizontal basis for students from PWD category.

About JNU

Ever wondered which University, the cadets from National Defence Academy (NDA) graduate from? Yes. It is Jawaharlal Nehru University (JNU). JNU started in the year 1969, three years after the act of Parliament in 1966. With several academic centres of JNU declared "Centres of Excellence" by the University Grants Commission, JNU has been ranked No. 1 by National Assessment and Accreditation Council (NAAC). JNU has been ranked No. 2 by National Institutional Ranking Framework (NIRF) 2020 and has been awarded the Best University Award by the President of India in 2017. The European Commission has awarded the Jean Monnet Centre of Excellence for European Union Studies in India (CEEUSI) to Jawaharlal Nehru University in 2018. This is one of the highest international recognition for any European Studies programme.

JNU was the first University to start integrated five-year Master of Arts in Language Courses. JNU actively collaborates with National and International Universities for student and faculty exchange programs.

According to university submissions for NIRF 2020, JNU has 1,048 students pursuing UG programs, of which 46 are foreign nationals.

JNU UG Programs

JNU offers a limited program at the undergraduate level, unlike other universities. The focus at undergraduate has been largely on language courses. In 2018, JNU started two programs in engineering and plans to add a few more specializations in future.

Please refer to the table below for the important undergraduate courses offered by JNU and the intake across each program.

School	Program	Intake	Duration
School of Language, Literature and Cultural Studies	B. A (Hons) Pashto	19	3 Years
	B. A (Hons) Persian	39	3 Years
	B. A (Hons) Arabic	39	3 Years
	B. A (Hons) Japanese	48	3 Years
	B. A (Hons) Korean	39	3 Years
	B. A (Hons) Chinese	44	3 Years
	B. A (Hons) French	48	3 Years
	B. A (Hons) German	48	3 Years
	B. A (Hons) Russian	68	3 Years
	B. A (Hons) Spanish	39	3 Years

School of Sanskrit and Indic Studies	B. Sc - M. Sc Integrated Program in Ayurveda Biology	20	5 Years
School of Engineering	B. Tech in Computer Science and Engineering & MS/M. Tech in Social Sciences/Humanities/Science/Technology	25	5 Years
	B. Tech in Electronics and Communication Engineering & MS/M. Tech in Social Sciences/Humanities/Science/Technology	25	5 Years

JNU UG Programs Eligibility:

Each of the courses have different eligibility for admissions. To be eligible for admissions, one must fulfil all the criteria as laid down by the respective faculties of the University.

B.A (Hons) Language Courses: Candidate must not be less than 17 years of age and must have passed Senior School Certificate (10+2) or equivalent examination with minimum of 45% marks.

B. Sc - M. Sc Integrated Program in Ayurveda Biology: Candidate must not be less than 17 years of age and must have passed Senior School Certificate (10+2) or equivalent examination with minimum of 45% marks.

B. Tech-M. Tech: Based on JEE Mains

JNU UG Admissions:

Until 2021, admissions to JNU UG courses were based on JNU Entrance Examination (JNUEE) conducted by the National Testing Agency (NTA). From the academic year 2022, admissions to UG programs offered by JNU will be based on CUET, which will replace the JNUEE. CUET will be a common entrance for admissions to UG programs offered by all the Central Universities in the country.

JNU UG Programs Reservation:

JNU being a Central University offers reservations in admissions according to central government rules.

Schedule Caste (SC): 15% of the total seats are reserved for students who belong to SC category.

Schedule Tribe (ST): 7.5% of the total seats are reserved for students belonging to ST Category.

Other Backward Classes (OBC): 27% of the total intake is reserved for students from Other Backward Classes (OBC), excluding those from creamy layer. Also, Central List of Caste to be followed.

Economically Weaker Section (EWS): The University has reserved 10% seats for EWS category, in accordance with the directive of Ministry of Education.

Persons with Disability (PWD): 5% of the seats are reserved on horizontal basis for students from PWD category.

About Jamia Milia Islamia

Jamia Milia Islamia (JMI) was founded in 1920 in Aligarh and became a Central University in 1988 by the act of Parliament. Jamia in Urdu stands for University and Milia means National, making Jamia Milia Islamia a National University. Jamia Milia Islamia moved to Delhi in 1925 and shifted to its present campus in Okhla in 1935.

Jamia Milia Islamia is a NAAC accredited University with grade "A" and was placed 10th in NIRF Rankings 2020. According to submissions made by University for NIRF 2021, Jamia Milia Islamia has a total of 5,911 students pursuing undergraduate courses at the University, of which 105 are foreign nationals. The University also manage to place a total of 681 UG students with an average salary ranging 4.2 Lacs-6.0 Lacs.

JMI UG Programs

Jamia Milia Islamia (JMI) offers a host of undergraduate programs for students. Through its various faculties, JMI offers a range of programs which caters to students learning abilities.

Please refer to the table below for the important undergraduate courses offered by Jamia Milia Islamia and the intake across each program.

Faculty	Course	Intake	Duration
Faculty of Humanities and Language	B. A (Hons) English	60	3 Years
	B. A (Hons) Hindi	40	3 Years
	B. A (Hons) Mass Media-Hindi	40	3 Years
	B. A (Hons) History	60	3 Years
	Bachelor of Hotel Management (BHM)	40	3 Years
	Bachelor of Tourism and Travel Management	40	3 Years
	B. Voc (Food Production)	40	3 Years
Faculty of Social Sciences	Bachelor of Arts (B. A)	68	3 Years
	B. Com (Hons)	55	3 Years
	BBA (Bachelor of Business Administration)	44	3 Years
	B. A (Hons) Economics	53	3 Years
	B. A (Hons) Sociology	42	3 Years
	B. A (Hons) Political Science	42	3 Years
	B. A (Hons) Psychology	42	3 Years
Faculty of Natural Sciences	B. Sc (Bachelor of Science)	50	3 Years
	B. Sc Biosciences	40	3 Years
	B. Sc Biotechnology	35	3 Years
	B. Sc (Hons) Chemistry	40	3 Years
	B. A/B. Sc (Hons) Geography	60	3 Years
	B. Sc (Hons) Mathematics	45	3 Years
	B. Sc (Hons) Applied Mathematics	45	3 Years
	B. Sc (Hons) Physics	45	3 Years
Faculty of Fine Arts	Bachelor of Fine Arts (Applied Art)	30	4 Years
	Bachelor of Fine Arts (Art Education)	20	4 Years
	Bachelor of Fine Arts (Painting)	20	4 Years
	Bachelor of Fine Arts (Sculpture)	10	4 Years

JMI UG Programs Eligibility:

Each of the courses have different eligibility for admissions. To be eligible for admissions, one must fulfil all the criteria as laid down by the respective faculties of the University.

B. Com (Hons) /BBA /B. A (Hons) Economics: Candidate must have passed class XII or equivalent with a minimum of 50% marks in five subjects.

BHM/BTTM/B. Voc (Food Production): Candidate must have passed class XII or equivalent with a minimum of 45% marks in five subjects.

B. A (Hons) Mass Media/B. A (Hons) Hindi: Candidate must have passed class XII or equivalent with a minimum of 45% marks in five subjects.

B. Sc/B. Sc (Hons): Candidate must have passed class XII or equivalent with minimum 50% marks in each of the science subjects i.e. Physics, Chemistry and Mathematics and 50% marks in aggregate of best 5-subjects.

JMI UG Admissions:

Until 2021, admissions to JMI UG courses were based on Entrance Test (JMI-ET) conducted by the University. From the academic year 2022, admissions to UG programs offered by JMI will be based on CUET, which will replace the JMI-ET. CUET will be a common entrance for admissions to UG programs offered by all the Central Universities in the country.

JMI UG Programs Reservation:

JMI is a minority reservation-based University and accordingly, seats are reserved for candidates as per the norms laid down by the University.

Muslim Minority: 30% of the total seats are reserved for Muslim applicants; 10% of the total seats are reserved for women applicants who are Muslim; 10% of the total intake is for OBC-NC candidates who are Muslims.

Persons with Disability (PWD): 5% of the seats are reserved for students from PWD category.

Jamia Students: 5% seats in all Undergraduate Programs shall be filled by internal students of Jamia who have passed their qualifying examination of the concerned programme (X or XII) from Jamia Schools as regular students.

In addition, Jamia Milia Islamia has supernumerary seats for Kashmiri Migrants and students from Jammu and Kashmir.

About Aligarh Muslim University

Aligarh Muslim University also referred as AMU was established by Sir Syed Ahmad Khan in 1875. The University started as Muhammadan Anglo-Oriental College and became a University (AMU) in 1920. The university has been ranked 801–1000 in the QS World University Rankings of 2021 and 17 in India by the National Institutional Ranking Framework in 2020.

Aligarh Muslim University is institution of national importance, under the seventh schedule of the Constitution of India.

AMU UG Programs

Aligarh Muslim University offers several programs at the undergraduate level. With 7 constituent colleges, the Aligarh Muslim University offers many undergraduate courses.

Please refer to the table below for the important undergraduate courses offered by the AMU and the intake across each program.

Course	Intake	Duration
B. Sc (Hons) Home Science	30*	3 Years
B.Sc (Hons) Agriculture	40	4 Years
B. A (Hons) Arabic	20+10*	3 Years
B. A (Hons) Communicative English	15+20*	3 Years
B. A (Hons) English	40+35*	3 Years
B. A (Hons) Hindi	40+25*	3 Years
B. A (Hons) Geography	50+20*	3 Years
B. A (Hons) Linguistics	20+25*	3 Years
B. A (Hons) Persian	15+25*	3 Years
B. A (Hons) Philosophy	20+10*	3 Years
B. A (Hons) Quaranic Studies	10+10*	3 Years
B. A (Hons) Sanskrit	15+10*	3 Years
B. A (Hons) Urdu	40+50*	3 Years
Bachelor of Fine Arts	15+15*	3 Years
B. Com (Hons)	180+100*	3 Years
B. Voc Production Technology	50	3 Years
B Voc Polymer and Coating Technology	50	3 Years
B. Voc Fashion Design and Garment Technology	50	3 Years
B. A (Hons) Chinese	20	3 Years
B. A (Hons) French	20	3 Years
B. A (Hons) German	20	3 Years

Program	Intake	Duration
B. A (Hons) Russian	20	3 Years
B. A (Hons) Spanish	20	3 Years
B. Sc (Hons) Biochemistry	30+30*	3 Years
B. Sc (Hons) Botany	60+40*	3 Years
B. Sc (Hons) Zoology	60+45*	3 Years
B. Sc (Hons) Physics	120+35*	3 Years
B. Sc (Hons) Chemistry	120+65*	3 Years
B. Sc (Hons) Mathematics	120+40*	3 Years
B. Sc (Hons) Geography	45+30*	3 Years
B. Sc (Hons) Geology	100+30*	3 Years
B. Sc (Hons) Statistics	60+30*	3 Years
B. Sc (Hons) Industrial Chemistry	20+10*	3 Years
B. Sc (Hons) Computer Applications	40+20*	3 Years

AMU UG Programs Eligibility:

As the University offers multiple programs and separate intake for male and female candidates, it is important to check the university official website regularly to keep oneself updated about the eligibility for each program, which can change.

AMU UG Admissions:

Until 2021, AMU conducted its own entrance test to admit students for the UG programs. From the academic year 2022, admissions to UG programs offered by Aligarh Muslim University will be based on CUET. CUET will be a common entrance for admissions to UG programs offered by all the Central Universities in the country.

University of Allahabad UG Programs Reservation:

Allahabad University being a Central University offers reservations in admissions according to central government rules. Kindly check the university website for further details.

GEOGRAPHY

PART – I

CHAPTER 1

Population Distribution, Density, Growth & Composition

India is the second most populous country after China in the world with its total population of 1,210 million (2011). India's population is larger than the total population of North America, South America and Australia put together.

Sources of Population Data

Population data are collected through Census operation held every 10 years in our country. The first population Census in India was conducted in 1872 but its first complete Census was conducted only in 1881.

Distribution of Population

The percentage shares of population of the states and Union Territories in the country show that Uttar Pradesh has the highest population followed by Maharashtra, Bihar and West Bengal.

An uneven spatial distribution of population in India suggests a close relationship between population and physical, socioeconomic and historical factor.

The North Indian Plains, deltas and Coastal Plains have higher proportion of population than the interior districts of southern and central Indian States, Himalayas, some of the north eastern and the western states.

Development of irrigation (Rajasthan), availability of mineral and energy resources (Jharkhand) and development of transport network (Peninsular States) have resulted in moderate to high concentration of population in areas which were previously very thinly populated.

It is observed that the regions falling in the river plains and coastal areas of India have remained the regions of larger population concentration.

On the other hand, the urban regions of Delhi, Mumbai, Kolkata, Bengaluru, Pune, Ahmedabad, Chennai and Jaipur have high concentration of population due to industrial development and urbanisation drawing a large numbers of rural-urban migrants.

Density of Population

The density of population in India (2011) is 382 persons per sq km. Among the northern Indian States, Bihar (1102), West Bengal (1029) and and Uttar Pradesh (828) have higher densities, while Kerala (859) and Tamil Nadu (555) have higher densities among the peninsular Indian states.

Growth of Population

The annual growth rate of India's population is 1.64 per cent (2011). There are four distinct phases of growth identified within this period:

Phase I: The period from 1901-1921 is referred to as a period of stagnant or stationary phase of growth of India's population, since in this period growth rate was very low, even recording a negative growth rate during 1911-1921.

Phase II: The decades 1921-1951 are referred to as the period of steady population growth. An overall improvement in health and sanitation throughout the country brought down the mortality rate.

Phase III: The decades 1951-1981 are referred to as the period of population explosion in India, which was caused by a rapid fall in the mortality rate but a high fertility rate of population in the country.

Phase IV: In the post 1981 till present, the growth rate of country's population though remained high, has started slowing down gradually.

Regional Variation in Population Growth

A continuous belt of states from west to east in the north-west, north, and north central parts of the country has relatively high growth rate than the southern states.

During 2001-2011, the growth rates of almost all States and Union Territories have registered a lower figure compared to the previous decade, namely, 1991-2001.

An important aspect of population growth in India is the growth of its adolescents. At present the share of adolescents i.e., up to the age group of 10-19 years is about 20.9 per cent (2011), among which male adolescents constitute 52.7 per cent and female adolescents constitute 47.3 per cent.

The National Youth Policy (NYP-2014) launched in February 2014 proposes a holistic 'vision' for the youth of India, which is "To empower the youth of the country to achieve their full potential, and through them enable India to find its rightful place in the community of nations".

Population Composition

Population composition is a distinct field of study within population geography with a vast coverage of analysis of age and sex, place of residence, ethnic characteristics, tribes, language, religion, marital status, literacy and education, occupational characteristics, etc.

Rural - Urban Composition: The states like Bihar and Sikkim have very high percentage of rural population. The states of Goa and Maharashtra have only little over half of their total population residing in villages.

A thorough examination of the pattern of distribution of rural population of India reveals that both at intra-State and interState levels, the relative degree of urbanization and extent of rural-urban migration regulate the concentration of rural population.

In the agriculturally stagnant parts of the middle and lower Ganga Plains, Telengana, non-irrigated Western Rajasthan, remote hilly, tribal areas of northeast, along the flood prone areas of Peninsular India and along eastern part of Madhya Pradesh, the degree of urbanisation has remained low.

Linguistic Composition: India is a land of linguistic diversity. According to Grierson (Linguistic Survey of India, 1903 - 1928), there were 179 languages and as many as 544 dialects in the country.

Among the scheduled languages, the speakers of Hindi have the highest percentage. The smallest language groups are Sanskrit, Bodo and Manipuri speakers (2011).

Religious composition: Religion is one of the most dominant forces affecting the cultural and political life of the majority of Indians. Hindus are distributed as a major group in many states (ranging from 70-90 per cent and above) except the districts of states along IndoBangladesh border, Indo-Pak border, Jammu & Kashmir, Hill States of North-East and in scattered areas of Deccan Plateau and Ganga Plain.

Muslims, the largest religious minority, are concentrated in Jammu & Kashmir, certain districts of West Bengal and Kerala, many districts of Uttar Pradesh, in and around Delhi and in Lakshadweep. They form majority in Kashmir valley and Lakshadweep.

The Christian population is distributed mostly in rural areas of the country. The main concentration is observed along the Western coast around Goa, Kerala and also in the hill states of Meghalaya, Mizoram, Nagaland, Chotanagpur area and Hills of Manipur.

Sikhs are mostly concentrated in relatively small area of the country, particularly in the states of Punjab, Haryana and Delhi.

Jains and Buddhists, the smallest religious groups in India have their concentration only in selected areas of the country. Jains have major concentration in the urban areas of Rajasthan, Gujarat and Maharashtra, while the Buddhists are concentrated mostly in Maharashtra.

Composition of Working Population: About 54.6 per cent of total working population are cultivators and agricultural labourers, whereas only 3.8% of workers are engaged in household industries and 41.6 % are other workers including non-household industries, trade, commerce, construction and repair and other services. As far as the occupation of country's male and female population is concerned, male workers out-number female workers in all the three sectors

Promoting Gender Sensitivity through 'Beti Bachao-Beti Padhao' Social Campaign: All efforts need to be made to address the denial of opportunities of education, employment, political representation, low wages for similar types of work, disregard to their entitlement to live a dignified life, etc. The Government of India has duly acknowledged the adverse impacts of these discriminations and launched a nationwide campaign called 'Beti Bachao - Beti Padhao'.

Exercise

1. In which year first population Census in India was conducted?
   - (a) 1882
   - (b) 1872
   - (c) 1883
   - (d) 1873

2. When the first complete census was conducted in India?
   - (a) 1881
   - (b) 1891
   - (c) 1871
   - (d) 1892

3. Which of the following state has the highest population?
   - (a) Bihar
   - (b) Uttar Pradesh
   - (c) Maharashtra
   - (d) Madhya Pradesh

4. In which state/UT share of population is very small?
   - (a) Jammu and Kashmir
   - (b) Arunachal Pradesh
   - (c) Uttarakhand
   - (d) Bihar

5. As per the census (2011) what was the density of population in India?
   - (a) 382 persons per sq km
   - (b) 482 persons per sq km
   - (c) 582 persons per sq km
   - (d) 682 persons per sq km

6. Which Indian state has highest densities?
   - (a) Uttar Pradesh
   - (b) Maharashtra
   - (c) Bihar
   - (d) West Bengal

7. Which of the options given below is correct about Agricultural density?
   - (a) total agricultural population / net cultivable area
   - (b) total agricultural crops / net cultivable area
   - (c) total agricultural village / net cultivable area
   - (d) total agricultural season / net cultivable area

8. What is the annual growth rate of India's population?
   - (a) 1.54 percent
   - (b) 1.64 percent
   - (c) 2 percent
   - (d) 2.4 percent

9. Which of the following period is known as stagnant phase of growth of population?
   - (a) 1921-1951
   - (b) 1901-1921
   - (c) 1900-1921
   - (d) 1902-1922

10. Which of the following decades is known as the period of population explosion in India?
    - (a) 1951-1981
    - (b) 1952-1982
    - (c) 1961-1971
    - (d) 1971-1981

11. When was National youth Policy passed in India?
    - (a) February 2014
    - (b) February 2015
    - (c) July 2014
    - (d) February 2013

12. According to NYP- 2014 ,youth is defined as________.
    - (a) as persons in the age group of 15-35 years.
    - (b) as persons in the age group of 12-29 years.
    - (c) as persons in the age group of 15-29 years.
    - (d) as persons in the age group of 15-59 years.

13. When National Policy was for Skill Development and Entrepreneurship, was passed in India?
    - (a) 2017
    - (b) 2016
    - (c) 2015
    - (d) 2019

14. What percent of total population of India live in village?
    - (a) 68.8 percent
    - (b) 75 percent
    - (c) 50 percent
    - (d) 45 percent

15. Which of the following is correct regarding Linguistic Survey of India?

    (a) 179 languages, 544 dialects

    (b) 100 languages, 544 dialects

    (c) 189 languages, 544 dialects

    (d) 199 languages, 544 dialects

16. Which of the following is the largest religious minority in India?

    (a) Christian   (b) Jain

    (c) Buddhism   (d) Muslim

17. Which of the following is defining Main worker?

    (a) Main Worker is a person who works for at least 183 days (or six months) in a year.

    (b) Main Worker is a person who works for more than 183 days (or six months) in a year.

    (c) Main Worker is a person who works for less than 183 days (or six months) in a year.

    (d) Main Worker is a person who works for atleast 362 days in a year.

18. "If development is not engendered it is endangered" statement was used by which international organization?

    (a) UNSC

    (b) UNDP

    (c) IMF

    (d) WTO

19. Which of the following is a crime against humanity?

    (a) Gender discrimination

    (b) Age discrimination

    (c) Religious discrimination

    (d) Region discrimination

20. Which of the following scheme was launched by government of India for decreasing gender discrimination?

    (a) 'Beti Bhagao - Beti Padhao'.

    (b) 'Beta Bachao - Beta Padhao'.

    (c) 'Laado Bachao - Laado Padhao'.

    (d) Ladki Bachao - Ladki Padhao'.

Answers

1. (b)	**2.** (a)	**3.** (b)	**4.** (b)	**5.** (a)	**6.** (c)	**7.** (a)	**8.** (b)	**9.** (b)	**10.** (a)
11. (a)	**12.** (c)	**13.** (c)	**14.** (a)	**15.** (a)	**16.** (d)	**17.** (a)	**18.** (b)	**19.** (a)	**20.** (a)

CHAPTER 2

Migration Types, Causes and Consequences

Migration has been an integral part and a very important factor in redistributing population over time and space. India has witnessed the waves of migrants coming to the country from Central and West Asia and also from Southeast Asia.

Large numbers of people from India too have been migrating to places in search of better opportunities specially to the countries of the Middle-East, Western Europe, America, Australia and East and South East Asia.

Migration: Actually migration was recorded beginning from the first Census of India conducted in 1881. This data were recorded on the basis of place of birth.

In the Census of India migration is enumerated on two bases :

(i) Place of birth, if the place of birth is different from the place of enumeration (known as life-time migrant)

(ii) Place of residence, if the place of last residence is different from the place of enumeration (known as migrant by place of last residence).

As per 2011 census, out of 1,210 million people in the country, 455.8 million (about 37%) were reported as migrants of place of last residence.

India also experiences immigration migration, four streams are identified:

(a) rural to rural (R-R);

(b) rural to urban (R-U);

(c) urban to urban (U-U); and

(d) urban to rural (U-R).

Indian Census 2011 has recorded that more than 5 million person have migrated to India from other countries. Out of these, about 88.9 per cent came from the neighboring countries: Bangladesh followed by Nepal and Pakistan.

Spatial Variation In Migration: Uttar Pradesh was the state, which had the largest number of net out-migrants from the state.

Causes of Migration: Reasons can be put into two broad categories:

(i) push factor, these cause people to leave their place of residence or origin; and

(ii) pull factors, which attract the people from different places.

In India people migrate from rural to urban areas mainly due to poverty, high population pressure on the land, lack of basic infrastructural facilities like health care, education, etc.

Work and employment have remained the main cause for male migration (26 per cent) while it is only 2.3 per cent for the females.

Consequences Of Migration

Consequences can be observed in economic, social, cultural, political and demographic terms.

Economic Consequences: Remittances from the international migrants are one of the major sources of foreign exchange. In 2002, India received US$ 11 billion as remittances from international migrants.

Demographic Consequences: Rural urban migration is one of the important factors contributing to the population growth of cities. Age and skill selective out migration from the rural area have adverse effect on the rural demographic structure.

Social Consequences: Migrants act as agents of social change. The new ideas related to new technologies, family planning, girl's education, etc. get diffused from urban to rural areas through them.

Environmental Consequences: Due to over-exploitation of natural resources, cities are facing the acute problem of depletion of ground water, air pollution, disposal of sewage and management of solid wastes.

Exercise

1. Which of the following is not the place where Indian migrants not move for better opportunities?
   - (a) Africa
   - (b) Middle-East
   - (c) Western Europe
   - (d) South East Asia

2. In which census for the first time actual migration was recorded?
   - (a) 1891
   - (b) 1871
   - (c) 1881
   - (d) 1861

3. What percent of the population of India was recorded as migrants as per 2011 census data?
   - (a) 39%
   - (b) 45%
   - (c) 25%
   - (d) 37%

4. Which of the following is not the one of the stream of immigration migration in India?
   - (a) urban to rural
   - (b) rural to urban
   - (c) urban to urban
   - (d) rural to rurban

5. Which of the following state have largest number of net out-migrants from the state?
   - (a) Uttar Pradesh
   - (b) Bihar
   - (c) Rajasthan
   - (d) Maharashtra

6. Which of the following will not come under push factor that causes migration?
   - (a) Drought
   - (b) Desertification
   - (c) Lack of employment opportunities
   - (d) Big Hospitals

7. Which of the following is the reason for migration from rural to urban areas?
   - (a) Poverty
   - (b) High population
   - (c) Lack of Health care
   - (d) All the above

8. Which of the following is the reason for large percentage migration of female in India?
   - (a) Marriage
   - (b) Employment
   - (c) Health
   - (d) Training

9. Which of the following are the economic consequences of migration in India?
   - (a) More FDI
   - (b) Remittance
   - (c) More FII
   - (d) High Inflation

10. Which of the following is a negative consequence of unregulated migration within the country?
    - (a) Development of slums
    - (b) Developments of City
    - (c) Development of Village
    - (d) Development of School

11. Which of the following are not the consequences of Migration in India?
    - (a) Migration leads to intermixing of people from diverse cultures.
    - (b) Migration leads to the redistribution of the population within a country
    - (c) Remittances sent by International migrants
    - (d) Decrease in Pollution

12. What is Girmit Act?
    - (a) Indian Emigration Act
    - (b) Permanent settlement in West Asia
    - (c) Government permission for rural to urban migration
    - (d) To ban migration

13. How many Indians migrated from India to other countries as per Census 2011?
    - (a) 5 million
    - (b) 4 million
    - (c) 3 million
    - (d) 6 million

14. What are the two major modifications was introduced in census 1961?
    - (a) place of birth
    - (b) duration of residence
    - (c) Information
    - (d) Both (a) and (b)

Answers

1. (a) **2.** (c) **3.** (d) **4.** (d) **5.** (a) **6.** (d) **7.** (d) **8.** (a) **9.** (b) **10.** (a)

11. (d) **12.** (a) **13.** (a) **14.** (d)

CHAPTER 3

Human Development

Apparently, it is believed that "Development is freedom" which is often associated with modernisation, leisure, comfort and affluence.

In the present context, computerisation, industrialisation, efficient transport and communication network, large education system, advanced and modern medical facilities, safety and security of individuals, etc. are considered as the symbols of development.

For India, development is a mixed bag of opportunities as well as neglect and deprivations. It is a well-established fact that majority of the scheduled castes, scheduled tribes, landless agricultural labourers, poor farmers and slums dwellers, etc. are the most marginalized lot.

The poor are being subjected to three inter-related processes of declining capabilities; i.e.

(1) social capabilities - due to displacement and weakening social ties (social capital),

(2) environmental capabilities - due to pollution and,

(3) personal capabilities - due to increasing incidence of diseases and accidents.

This, in turn, has adverse effects on their quality of life and human development.

What is Human Development?

"Human development is a process of enlarging the range of people's choices, increasing their opportunities for education, health care, income and empowerment and covering the full range of human choices from a sound physical environment to economic, social and political freedom."

Thus, enlarging the range of people's choices is the most significant aspect of human development. People's choices may involve a host of other issues, but, living a long and healthy life, to be educated and have access to resources needed for a decent standard of living including political freedom, guaranteed human rights and personal self-respect, etc. are considered some of the non-negotiable aspects of the human development

---

Concerted efforts were made to look at development critically at various times in the past. But, most systematic effort towards this was the publication of the First Human Development Report by United Nations Development Programme (UNDP) in 1990.

According to the Human Development Report 1993, "progressive democratisation and increasing empowerment of people are seen as the minimum conditions for human development". Moreover, it also mentions that "development must be woven around people, not the people around development" as was the case previously.

Human Development in India

India with a population of over 1.20 billion is ranked 130 among 189 countries of the world in terms of the Human Development Index (HDI). With the composite HDI value of 0.640 India finds herself grouped with countries showing medium human development.

Low scores in the HDI is a matter of serious concern but, some reservations have been expressed about the approach as well as indicators selected to calculate the index values and ranking of the states/countries.

Using the indicators selected by the UNDP, the Planning Commission of India also prepared the Human Development Report for India. It used states and the Union Territories as the units of analysis. Subsequently, each state government also started preparing the state level Human Development Reports, using districts as the units of analysis.

Indicators of Economic Attainments

Gross National Product (GNP) and its per capita availability are taken as measures to assess the resource base/ endowment of any country. Economic attainment and the well-being of individuals depend on economic growth, employment opportunities and access to assets.

The percentage of persons below the poverty line in 2011-12 has been estimated as 25.7% in rural areas, 13.7% in urban areas and 21.9% for the country as a whole.

The Gross Domestic Product (GDP) of a country does not fully reflect the quality of life of a country. There are other factors like housing, access to public transport, air, quality and access to drinking water which also determine the standard of living. Jobless growth and rampant unemployment are some of the important reasons for higher incidences of poverty in India.

Indicators of a Healthy Life

Availability of pre and post natal healthcare facilities in order to reduce infant mortality and post-delivery deaths among mothers, old age health care, adequate nutrition and safety of individual are some important measures of a healthy and reasonably long life.

India has done reasonably well in some of the health indicators like decline in death rate from 25.1 per thousand in 1951 to 6.5 per thousand in 2015 and infant mortality from 148 per thousand to 37 during the same period. Similarly, it also succeeded in increasing life expectancy at birth from 37.1 years to 66.9 years for males and 36.2 to 70 years for females from 1951 to 2015.

India has recorded declining female sex ratio. The findings of 2011 Census of India are very disturbing particularly in case of child sex ratio in the age group of 0-6 years.

The other significant features of the report are, with the exception of Kerala, the child sex ratio has declined in all the states and it is the most alarming in the developed state of Haryana and Punjab where it is below 850 female children per thousand male children.

Indicators of Social Empowerment

"Development is freedom". Freedom from hunger, poverty, servitude, bondage, ignorance, illiteracy and any other forms of domination is the key to human development.

Access to knowledge about the society and environment are fundamental to freedom. Literacy is the beginning of access to such a world of knowledge and freedom.

Human Development Index in India

There are several socio-political, economic and historical reasons for such a state of affairs. Kerala is able to record the highest value in the HDI largely due to its impressive performance in achieving near hundred per cent literacy.

In a different scenario the states like Bihar, Madhya Pradesh, Odisha, Assam and Uttar Pradesh have very low literacy. States showing higher total literacy rates have less gaps between the male and female literacy rates.

Population, Environment and Development

Development in general and human development in particular is a complex concept used in social sciences. It is complex because for ages it was thought that development is a substantive concept and once it is achieved it will address all the socio-cultural and environmental ills of the society.

Considering the gravity and sensitivity of the issues involved, the UNDP in its Human Development Report 1993, tried to amend some of the implicit biases and prejudices which were entrenched in the concept of development.

The report recognised greater constructive role of 'Civil Societies' in bringing about peace and human development. The civil society should work for building up opinion for reduction in the military expenditure, demobilisation of armed forces, transition from defence to production of basic goods and services and particularly disarmament and reduction in the nuclear warheads by the developed countries.

Scholar like Sir Robert Malthus was the first one to voice his concern about the growing scarcity of resources as compared to the human population.

Indian culture and civilisation have been very sensitive to the issues of population, resource and development for a long time. It would not be incorrect to say that the ancient scriptures were essentially concerned about the balance and harmony among the elements of nature.

His views were also re-echoed in the Club of Rome Report "Limits to Growth" (1972), Schumacher's book "Small is Beautiful" (1974), Brundtland Commission's Report "Our Common Future" (1987) and finally in the "Agenda-21 Report of the Rio Conference" (1993).

Exercise

1. Which of the following organization published Human Development report?

   (a) UNCTAD   (b) UNEP

   (c) UNDP   (d) UNFCCC

2. What is the Human Development Index of India?

   (a) 0.640   (b) 0.840

   (c) 0.940   (d) 0.740

3. Which of the following organization in India also prepare Human Development report?

   (a) Ministry of Human Resource development

   (b) Planning commission

   (c) Ministry of Finance

   (d) Ministry of Home affairs

4. Which of the following is reason for decline in the proportion of population living below the poverty line?

   (a) Only per capita income increases

   (b) Expenditure not increases

   (c) the per capita income and consumption expenditure increases

   (d) decline in inflation

5. What percentage of population in India is below poverty line as per 2011-12 data?

   (a) 41.9%   (b) 29.9%

   (c) 31.9%   (d) 21.9%

6. Which of the following is an important reasons for higher incidences of poverty in India?

   (1) Jobless growth

   (2) Rampant unemployment

   (3) More FDI in India

   (4) Decrease in Population

   Select the correct answer using the codes given below:

   (a) 1 and 2 only   (b) 2 and 3 only

   (c) 1,2 and 3   (d) 1 and 4 only

7. Which of the following are not the objectives of Swachh Bharat Mission (SBM)?

   (1) making India open defecation-free

   (2) making provisions for the supply of clean energy fuel LPG

   (3) promoting the use of non-convention energy

   Select the correct answer using the codes given below:

   (a) 1 and 3 only   (b) 1 and 2 only

   (c) 1, 2 and 3   (d) 2 and 3 only

8. What is the death rate data in India?

   (a) 6.5 per thousand   (b) 8.5 per thousand

   (c) 9.5 per thousand   (d) 105 per thousand

9. What is the present life expectancy at birth in India for both male and female?

   (a) 66.9 years for males and 70 years for females

   (b) 66.9 years for males and 60 years for females

   (c) 66.9 years for males and 50 years for females

   (d) 66.9 years for males and 80 years for females

10. What is the total literacy rate in India as per census 2011?

    (a) 74.04 per cent (2011)

    (b) 64.04 per cent (2011)

    (c) 54.04 per cent (2011)

    (d) 84.04 per cent (2011)

11. When was the first Human Development Report published by the UNDP?

    (a) 1970   (b) 1980

    (c) 1990   (d) 1995

12. Which of the following state have highest HDI in India?

    (a) Tamil Nadu   (b) Kerala

    (c) Bihar   (d) Gujrat

13. Which one of the following states of India has the lowest female literacy?

    (a) Jammu and Kashmir   (b) Bihar

    (c) Jharkhand   (d) Gujrat

Answers

1. (c)   **2.** (a)   **3.** (b)   **4.** (c)   **5.** (d)   **6.** (a)   **7.** (c)   **8.** (a)   **9.** (a)   **10.** (a)

11. (c)   **12.** (b)   **13.** (b)

Your Notes :

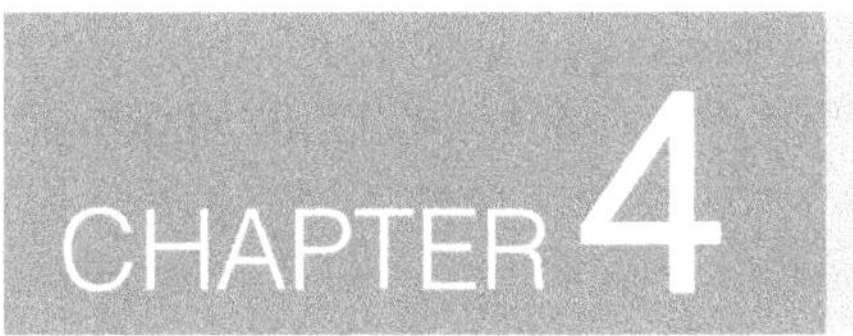

Human Settlements

Human Settlement means cluster of dwellings of any type or size where human beings live. Settlements vary in size and type. They range from a hamlet to metropolitan cities. Settlements could be small and sparsely spaced; they may also be large and closely spaced.

Rural Settlement	Urban Settlement
The rural settlements derive their life support or basic economic needs from land based primary economic activities.	• Urban settlements, depend on processing of raw materials and manufacturing of finished goods on the one hand and a variety of services on the other.
Rural people are less mobile and therefore, social relations among them are intimate.	• In urban areas, on the other hand, way of life is complex and fast, and social relations are formal.

Types of of Rural Settlement

There are various factors and conditions responsible for having different types of rural settlements in India.

(i) physical features - nature of terrain, altitude, climate and availability of water

(ii) cultural and ethenic factors - social structure, caste and religion

(iii) security factors - defence against thefts and robberies.

Rural Settlements in India can Broadly be put into Four Types:

- Clustered, agglomerated or nucleated,
- Semi-clustered or fragmented,
- Hamleted, and
- Dispersed or isolated.

Clustered Settlements: The clustered rural settlement is a compact or closely built up area of houses. Such settlements are generally found in fertile alluvial plains and in the northeastern states

Sometimes, people live in compact village for security or defence reasons, such as in the Bundelkhand region of central India and in Nagaland.

Semi-Clustered Settlements: Semi-clustered or fragmented settlements may result from tendency of clustering in a restricted area of dispersed settlement. More often such a pattern may also result from segregation or fragmentation of a large compact village.

Such settlements are widespread in the Gujarat plain and some parts of Rajasthan.

Hamleted Settlements: Sometimes settlement is fragmented into several units physically separated from each other bearing a common name. These units are locally called panna, para, palli, nagla, dhani, etc. in various parts of the country.

Dispersed Settlements: Dispersed or isolated settlement pattern in India appears in the form of isolated huts or hamlets of few huts in remote jungles, or on small hills with farms or pasture on the slopes.

Urbanisation in India

The level of urbanisation is measured in terms of percentage of urban population to total population. The level of urbanisation in India in 2011 was 31.16 per cent, which is quite low in comparison to developed countries.

Functional Classification of Towns

Administrative towns and cities Towns supporting administrative headquarters of higher order are administrative towns, such as Chandigarh, New Delhi, Bhopal, Shillong, Guwahati.

Industrial towns Industries constitute prime motive force of these cities, such as Mumbai, Salem, Coimbatore, Modinagar, Jamshedpur.

Transport Cities They may be ports primarily engaged in export and import activities such as Kandla, Kochchi, Kozhikode, Vishakhapatnam, etc

Commercial towns Towns and cities specialising in trade and commerce are kept in this class. Kolkata, Saharanpur, Satna, etc., are some examples.

Mining towns These towns have developed in mineral rich areas such as Raniganj, Jharia, Digboi, Ankaleshwar, Singrauli, etc.

Garrisson Cantonment towns These towns emerged as garrisson towns such as Ambala, Jalandhar, Mhow, Babina, Udhampur, etc.

Smart Cities Mission

The objective of the Smart Cities Mission is to promote cities that provide core infrastructure, a clean and sustainable environment and give a decent quality of life to its citizens. One of the features of Smart Cities is to apply smart solutions to infrastructure and services in order to make them better.

Exercise

1. The rural settlements derive their life support or basic economic needs from________.
   (a) Processing of raw materials
   (b) Land based economic activities
   (c) Manufacturing
   (d) Service

2. Which of the following are not the factors responsible for having different types of rural settlements in India?
   (a) caste and religion
   (b) nature of terrain
   (c) defe nce against thefts
   (d) Technology

3. Which type of rural settlement is found in fertile alluvial plains of India?
   (a) Clustered Settlements
   (b) Hamleted Settlements
   (c) Dispersed Settlements
   (d) Semi-Clustered Settlements

4. What is the reason for compact settlements in Rajasthan villages?
   (a) Defense
   (b) Wild animals
   (c) Scarcity of water
   (d) Soil erosion

5. Which one of the rural settlements also known as panna, para, palli etc?
   (a) Dispersed Settlements
   (b) Hamleted Settlements
   (c) Clustered settlements
   (d) Semi-clustered settlements

6. Which of the following are not the examples of Ancient town?
   (a) Varanasi
   (b) Madurai
   (c) Nagpur
   (d) Prayag

7. Which one of the following towns is not the example of fort town?
   (a) Hyderabad
   (b) Jaipur
   (c) Chennai
   (d) Agra

8. Which of the following town is a Satellite town?
   (a) Ghaziabad
   (b) Rohtak
   (c) Gurugram
   (d) Bhilai

9. What was the level of urbanization in India in 2011?
   (a) 31.16 per cent
   (b) 41.16 per cent
   (c) 21.16 per cent
   (d) 61.16 per cent

10. Which of the following combinations not consist of urban agglomeration?
    (a) a town and its adjoining urban outgrowths
    (b) two or more contiguous towns with or without their outgrowths
    (c) a village near to town
    (d) a city and one or more adjoining towns with their outgrowths together forming a contiguous spread

11. What percentage of population of India lives in Class 1 towns?
    (a) 50 percent
    (b) 60 percent
    (c) 40 percent
    (d) 30 percent

12. Which of the following city is largest agglomeration in India?
    (a) Delhi
    (b) Kolkata
    (c) Greater Mumbai
    (d) Chennai

13. Which of the following towns is not an example of Mining towns?
    (a) Raniganj
    (b) Jharia
    (c) Bhilai
    (d) Ankaleshwar

14. Which of the following town is an example of Educational town?
    (a) Pushkar
    (b) Tirupati
    (c) Madurai
    (d) Allahabad

15. Which of the following are not the objectives of Smart City Mission?
    (a) a clean and sustainable environment
    (b) decent quality of life to its citizens
    (c) smart solutions to infrastructure
    (d) promotion of more industries in urban areas

Answers

1. (b) **2.** (d) **3.** (a) **4.** (c) **5.** (b) **6.** (c) **7.** (c) **8.** (d) **9.** (a) **10.** (c)

11. (b) **12.** (c) **13.** (c) **14.** (d) **15.** (d)

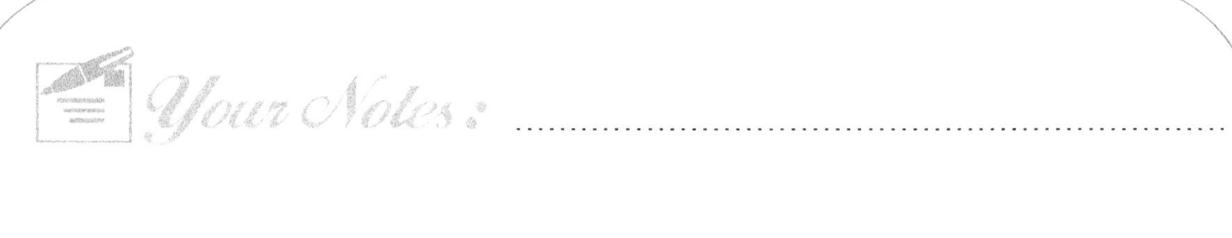

Your Notes :

CHAPTER 5

Land Resources and Agriculture

Land Use Categories

Land-use records are maintained by land revenue department.

The land-use categories as maintained in the Land Revenue Records are as follows :

Forests

It is important to note that area under actual forest cover is different from area classified as forest. The latter is the area which the Government has identified and demarcated for forest growth. The land revenue records are consistent with the latter definition. Thus, there may be an increase in this category without any increase in the actual forest cover.

Barren and Wastelands

The land which may be classified as a wasteland such as barren hilly terrains, desert lands, ravines, etc. normally cannot be brought under cultivation with the available technology.

Land-use Changes in India

India has undergone major changes within the economy over the past four or five decades, and this has influenced the land-use changes in the country.

There are two points that you need to remember before you derive some meaning from this figure. Firstly, the percentages shown in the figure have been derived with respect to the reporting area. Secondly, since even the reporting area has been relatively constant over the years, a decline in one category usually leads to an increase in some other category.

The four categories that have registered a decline are barren and wasteland, culturable wasteland, area under pastures and tree crops and fallow lands.

Common Property Resources

CPR is owned by the state meant for the use of the community. CPRs provide fodder for the livestock and fuel for the households along with other minor forest products like fruits, nuts, fibre, medicinal plants, etc.

In rural areas, such land is of particular relevance for the livelihood of the landless and marginal farmers and other weaker sections since many of them depend on income from their livestock due to the fact that they have limited access to land.

Agricultural Land Use in India

Land resource is more crucial to the livelihood of the people depending on agriculture:

Agriculture is a purely land based activity unlike secondary and tertiary activities. Contribution of land in agricultural output is more compared to its contribution in the outputs in the other sectors.

There has been a greater decline of cultivated land, in spite of a corresponding decline of cultivable wasteland.

Cropping Seasons in India

There are three distinct crop seasons in the northern and interior parts of country, namely kharif, rabi and zaid.

Cropping Season	Major Crops Cultivated	
	Northern States	**Southern States**
Karif June-September	Rice, Cotton, Bajra, Maize, Jowar, Tur	Rice, Maize, Ragi, Jowar, Groundnut
Rabi October-March	Weat, Gram, Rapeseeds and Mustard, Barely	Rice, Maize, Ragi, Groundnut, Jowar
Zaid April-June	Vegetables, Fruiits, Fodder	Rice, Vegetables, Fodder

Types of Farming

Rainfed farming is further classified on the basis of adequacy of soil moisture during cropping season into dryland and wetland farming. In India, the dryland farming is largely confined to the regions having annual rainfall less than 75 cm.

In wetland farming, the rainfall is in excess of soil moisture requirement of plants during rainy season. Such regions may face flood and soil erosion hazards.

Foodgrains

On the basis of the structure of grain the foodgrains are classified as cereals and pulses.

Cereals The cereals occupy about 54 per cent of total cropped area in India. The country produces about 11 per cent cereals of the world and ranks third in production after China and U.S.A.

India produces a variety of cereals, which are classified as fine grains (rice, wheat) and coarse grains (jowar, bajra, maize, ragi), etc

Rice: Rice is a staple food for the overwhelming majority of population in India. These are successfully grown from sea level to about 2,000 m altitude and from humid areas in eastern India to dry but irrigated areas of Punjab, Haryana, western U.P. and northern Rajasthan.

In West Bengal farmers grow three crops of rice called 'aus', 'aman' and 'boro'. About one-fourth of the total cropped area in the country is under rice cultivation. Punjab and Haryana are not traditional rice growing areas.

Wheat: Wheat is the second most important cereal crop in India after rice. India produces about 12.3 per cent of total wheat production of world (2016). About 14 per cent of the total cropped area in the country is under wheat cultivation.

Jowar: The coarse cereals together occupy about 16.50 per cent of total cropped area in the country. Among these, jowar or sorghum alone accounts for about 5.3 per cent of total cropped area.

Bajra: Bajra is sown in hot and dry climatic conditions in northwestern and western parts of the country. Leading producers of bajra are the states of Maharashtra, Gujarat, Uttar Pradesh, Rajasthan and Haryana.

Maize: Maize is a food as well as fodder crop grown under semi-arid climatic conditions and over inferior soils.It is high in southern states and declines towards central parts.

Pulses: Pulses are a very important ingredient of vegetarian food as these are rich sources of proteins. Pulses occupy about 11 per cent of the total cropped area in the country. Gram and tur are the main pulses cultivated in India.

Gram: Gram is cultivated in subtropical areas. It is mostly a rainfed crop cultivated during rabi season in central, western and northwestern parts of the country.

Tur (Arhar): Tur is the second important pulse crop in the country. It is also known as red gram or pigeon pea. This crop occupies only about 2 per cent of total cropped area of India.

Oilseeds: The oilseeds are produced for extracting edible oils. These crops together occupy about 14 per cent of total cropped area in the country.

Groundnut: India produces about 16.6 per cent of the total groundnut production in the world (2016). It is largely a rainfed kharif crop of drylands. It covers about 3.6 per cent of total cropped area in the country.

Rapeseed and Mustard: Rapeseed and mustard comprise several oilseeds as rai, sarson, toria and taramira. These oilseeds together occupy only about 2.5 per cent of total cropped area in the country.Rajasthan contributes about one-third production while other leading producers are Haryana and Madhya Pradesh.

Fibre Crops

Cotton: Cotton is a tropical crop grown in kharif season in semi-arid areas of the country. India lost a large proportion of cotton growing area to Pakistan during partition.

Jute: Jute is used for making coarse cloth, bags, sacks and decorative items. It is a cash crop in West Bengal and adjoining eastern parts of the country.Bihar and Assam are other jute growing areas.

Other Crops

Sugarcane: Sugarcane is a crop of tropical areas. Under rainfed conditions, it is cultivated in sub-humid and humid climates. In Indo-Gangetic plain, its cultivation is largely concentrated in Uttar Pradesh.India was the second largest producer of sugarcane after Brazil in 2015.

Tea: Tea is a plantation crop used as beverage. Black tea leaves are fermented whereas green tea leaves are unfermented. Tea leaves have rich content of caffeine and tannin. India is a leading producer of tea and accounts for about 21.1 per cent of total production in the world 2016.

Coffee: Coffee is a tropical plantation crop. Its seeds are roasted, ground and are used for preparing a beverage. There are three varieties of coffee i.e. arabica, robusta and liberica.

Agricultural Development in India

After Independence, the immediate goal of the Government was to increase foodgrains production by (i) switching over from cash crops to food crops; (ii) intensification of cropping over already cultivated land; and (iii) increasing cultivated area by bringing cultivable and fallow land under plough.

To overcome this problem, Intensive Agricultural District Programme (IADP) and Intensive Agricultural Area Programme (IAAP) were launched.

Spurt of agricultural growth came to be known as 'Green Revolution'. This also gave fillip to the development of a large number of agro-inputs, agro-processing industries and small-scale industries.

The Planning Commission of India focused its attention on the problems of agriculture in rainfed areas in 1980s.

National Mission for Sustainable Agriculture (NMSA)

National Mission for Sustainable Agriculture is to make agriculture more productive, sustainable, remunerative and climate resilient by promoting location specific integrated/ composite farming systems and to conserve natural resources through appropriate soil and moisture conservation measures.

Problems of Indian Agricultur Riculturriculture

Dependence on erratic monsoon: Irrigation covers only about 33 per cent of the cultivated area in India. The crop production in rest of the cultivated land directly depends on rain. Droughts and floods continue to be the twin menace in Indian agriculture.

Low productivity: The yield of the crops in the country is low in comparison to the international level. Per hectare output of most of the crops such as rice, wheat, cotton and oilseeds in India is much lower than that of the U.S.A., Russia and Japan.

Constraints of Financial Resources and Indebtedness

The inputs of modern agriculture are very expensive. This resource intensive approach has become unmanageable for marginal and small farmers as they have very meagre or no saving to invest in agriculture.

Lack of Land Reforms

Indian peasantry had been exploited for a long time as there had been unequal distribution of land.

Small Farm Size and Fragmentation of Landholdings: There are a large number of marginal and small farmers in the country. The average size of land holding is shrinking under increasing population pressure.

Lack of Commercialisation: A large number of farmers produce crops for self-consumption. These farmers do not have enough land resources to produce more than their requirement.

Vast Underemployment: There is a massive underemployment in the agricultural sector in India, particularly in the unirrigated tracts. In these areas, there is a seasonal unemployment ranging from 4 to 8 months.

Degradation of Cultivable Land: One of the serious problems that arises out of faulty strategy of irrigation and agricultural development is degradation of land resources. This is serious because it may lead to depletion of soil fertility.

Exercise

1. Which one of the following is responsible for measuring geographical area of administrative units in India?
   - (a) Indian council of agriculture research
   - (b) Survey of India
   - (c) Department of earth science
   - (d) Geology of India

2. Which one of the following is not the example of Barren or wasteland in India?
   - (a) Desert land
   - (b) Hilly terrain
   - (c) Flood plain
   - (d) Ravines

3. The land which is left without cultivation for one or less than one agricultural year is called___________.
   - (a) Culturable wasteland
   - (b) Current fallow
   - (c) Grazing land
   - (d) Pasture land

4. How many years land is left fallow to be called Culturable wasteland?
   - (a) More than 6 years
   - (b) More than 8 years
   - (c) More than 2 years
   - (d) More than 5years

5. Which of the following types of changes not affect land use in the country?
   - (a) size of the economy
   - (b) the composition of the economy
   - (c) contribution of the agricultural activities
   - (d) Biodiversity

6. Which of the following is reason for decline of pastures and grazing land?
   - (a) Illegal encroachment
   - (b) Forest fires
   - (c) Use of chemical fertilizers
   - (d) Soil erosion

7. Which one of the following is not a kharif crops?
   - (a) Rice
   - (b) Cotton
   - (c) Jute
   - (d) Mustard

8. Watermelons, cucumbers, vegetables are grown in which season of the year?
   - (a) Kharif
   - (b) Rabi
   - (c) Zaid
   - (d) Monsoon

9. Which one of the following region of India have dryland farming?
   - (a) regions having annual rainfall less than 200 cm
   - (b) regions having annual rainfall more than 75 cm
   - (c) regions having annual rainfall between 250-300 cm
   - (d) regions having annual rainfall less than 75 cm

10. Which one of the following is not the example of Drought resistant crops?
    - (a) Ragi
    - (b) Wheat
    - (c) Moong
    - (d) Bajra

11. Which one of the following is not a water intensive crops?
    - (a) Rice
    - (b) Jute
    - (c) Sugarcane
    - (d) Guar

12. What percent of world production India produces cereals?
    - (a) 11 per cent
    - (b) 21 per cent
    - (c) 51 per cent
    - (d) 10 per cent

13. Which one of the following is an example of coarse grain?
    - (a) Rice
    - (b) Wheat
    - (c) Coffee
    - (d) Bajra

14. Tea is an indigenous crop of which country?
    - (a) Malaysia
    - (b) South Africa
    - (c) Brazil
    - (d) China

15. Arabica, robusta and liberica are varieties of which crop?

    (a) Tea

    (b) Pulses

    (c) Coffee

    (d) Millets

16. Which one of the following state is leading producer of coffee in India?

    (a) Tamil Nadu

    (b) Kerala

    (c) Karnataka

    (d) Maharashtra

17. What is the world rank of India in sugarcane production?

    (a) First

    (b) Second

    (c) Third

    (d) Fourth

18. Which one of the following crop area was lost by India during partition?

    (a) Coffee

    (b) Cotton

    (c) Sugarcane

    (d) Tea

19. Which one of the following state is a leading producer of Jute?

    (a) West Bengal

    (b) Bihar

    (c) Orissa

    (d) Jharkhand

20. Which one of the following is not the problem of Indian agriculture?

    (a) Low productivity

    (b) Lack of Land Reforms

    (c) High Growth rate

    (d) Degradation of Cultivable Land

Answers

1. (b)   **2.** (c)   **3.** (b)   **4.** (d)   **5.** (d)   **6.** (a)   **7.** (d)   **8.** (c)   **9.** (d)   **10.** (b)

11. (d)   **12.** (a)   **13.** (d)   **14.** (d)   **15.** (c)   **16.** (c)   **17.** (b)   **18.** (b)   **19.** (a)   **20.** (c)

Your Notes:

Water Resources

Water is a cyclic resource with abundant supplies on the globe. Approximately, 71 per cent of the earth's surface is covered with it but freshwater constitutes only about 3 per cent of the total water.

Water Resources of India

India accounts for about 2.45 per cent of the world's surface area, 4 per cent of the world's water resources and about 16 per cent of the world's population. The total utilizable water resource in the country is only 1,122 cubic km.

Surface Water Resources

There are four major sources of surface water. These are rivers, lakes, ponds and tanks. Given that precipitation is relatively high in the catchment areas of the Ganga, the Brahmaputra and the Barak rivers, these rivers, although account for only about one-third of the total area in the country, have 60 per cent of the total surface water resources.

Groundwater Resources

The total replenishable groundwater resources in the country are about 432 cubic km. The groundwater utilisation is very high in the states of Punjab, Haryana, Rajasthan, and Tamil Nadu. If the present trend continues, the demands for water would need the supplies.

Lagoons and Backwaters

The States like Kerala, Odisha and West Bengal have vast surface water resources in these lagoons and lakes. Although, water is generally brackish in these water bodies, it is used for fishing and irrigating certain varieties of paddy crops, coconut, etc

Water Demand and Utilisation

Agriculture accounts for most of the surface and groundwater utilisation, it accounts for 89 per cent of the surface water and 92 per cent of the groundwater utilization.

Demand of Water for Irrigation

The large tracts of the country are deficient in rainfall and are drought prone. North-western India and Deccan plateau constitute such areas. Provision of irrigation makes multiple cropping possible. It has also been found that irrigated lands have higher agricultural productivity than unirrigated land. In Punjab, Haryana and western Uttar Pradesh, more than 85 per cent of their net sown area is under irrigation.

The over-use of groundwater resources has led to decline in groundwater table in these states.

Emerging Water Problems

The per capita availability of water is dwindling day-by-day due to increase in population.

Deterioration of Water Quality

Water quality refers to purity of water, or water without unwanted foreign substances. Water gets polluted by foreign matters, such as micro-organisms, chemicals, industrial and other wastes.

Water Conservation and Management

Besides developing water-saving technologies and methods, attempts are also to be made to prevent the pollution.

Prevention of Water Pollution

The Central Pollution Control Board (CPCB) in collaboration with State Pollution Control Boards has been monitoring water quality of national aquatic resources at 507 stations. The legislative provisions such as the Water (Prevention and Control of Pollution) Act 1974, and Environment Protection Act 1986 have not been implemented effectively.

Recycle and Reuse of Water

Use of water of lesser quality such as reclaimed wastewater would be an attractive option for industries for cooling and fire fighting to reduce their water cost.

Watershed Management

Watershed management basically refers to efficient management and conservation of surface and groundwater resources.

Haryali is a watershed development project sponsored by the Central Government which aims at enabling the rural population to conserve water for drinking, irrigation, fisheries and afforestation. Neeru-Meeru (Water and You) programme (in Andhra Pradesh) and Arvary Pani Sansad (in Alwar, Rajasthan) have taken up constructions of various water-harvesting structures such as percolation tanks, dug out ponds (Johad), check dams, etc., through people's participation.

Rainwater Harvesting

Rainwater harvesting is a method to capture and store rainwater for various uses. It is also used to recharge groundwater aquifers. Rainwater harvesting has been practised through various methods by different communities in the country for a long time. There is a wide scope to use rainwater harvesting technique to conserve precious water resource.

Exercise

1. What percent of freshwater available on the earth to the total water?
   - (a) 5 percent
   - (b) 3 percent
   - (c) 10 percent
   - (d) 8 percent

2. How much total utilizable water resource available in the country?
   - (a) 1,122 cubic km.
   - (b) 122 cubic km.
   - (c) 1,000 cubic km.
   - (d) 3,122 cubic km.

3. Which one of the following state groundwater utilization is not very high?
   - (a) Punjab
   - (b) Haryana
   - (c) Kerala
   - (d) Tamil Nadu

4. Which one of the following state lagoon is not found?
   - (a) West Bengal
   - (b) Odisha
   - (c) Kerala
   - (d) Bihar

5. Which one of the following is a multipurpose river project in India?
   - (a) Bhakra-Nangal
   - (b) Damodar Valley
   - (c) Indira Gandhi Canal Project
   - (d) All the above

6. The highest proportion of the total water used in the country is in which one of the following sectors?
   - (a) Agriculture
   - (b) Industry
   - (c) Domestic use
   - (d) Transport

7. Which one of the following is not the aim of Haryali Project?
   - (a) Irrigation
   - (b) Fisheries
   - (c) Afforestation
   - (d) Electricity production

8. Which one of the following organization monitoring water quality of country?
   - (a) Central Pollution control Board
   - (b) National green tribunal
   - (c) Supreme court
   - (d) Ministry of Agriculture

9. Which river of India is most polluted?
   - (a) Ganga
   - (b) Yamuna
   - (c) Kaveri
   - (d) Godavari

10. In which year water cess act came into force in India?
    - (a) 1997
    - (b) 1987
    - (c) 1977
    - (d) 1967

11. Which one of the following toxic metal found in Indian groundwater?
    - (a) Sodium
    - (b) Lead
    - (c) Cadmium
    - (d) Arsenic

12. Which of the following states, where concentration of Arsenic in groundwater is increased?
    - (a) Bihar
    - (b) West Bengal
    - (c) Rajasthan
    - (d) Both A and B

13. In which of the following state green revolution was not success?
    - (a) Punjab
    - (b) Haryana
    - (c) Maharashtra
    - (d) Uttar Pradesh

14. Which parts of India is drought prone?
    - (a) North India
    - (b) North West
    - (c) Eastern India
    - (d) Coastal States

15. Which of the following state is highest use of irrigation in India?

(a) Punjab

(b) Haryana

(c) Uttar Pradesh

(d) Bihar

16. What is the reason for increased in concentration of toxic metals in groundwater?

(a) Pollution

(b) Rainfall

(c) Over-use of groundwater

(d) Urbanization

17. Which one of the following is the reason for increasing salinity in the soil of Punjab and Haryana?

(a) High rainfall

(b) Large industries

(c) Domestic use of water

(d) Intensive irrigation

18. What percent of the total water available in India is beneficial use?

(a) 60 percent

(b) 50 percent

(c) 40 percent

(d) 30 percent

19. Which of the surface water in India is brackish?

(a) River

(b) Lakes

(c) Pond

(d) Lagoon

20. Which of the following crops required more water for cultivation?

(a) Rice

(b) Jute

(c) Sugarcane

(d) All the above

Answers

1. (b)	**2.** (a)	**3.** (c)	**4.** (d)	**5.** (d)	**6.** (a)	**7.** (d)	**8.** (a)	**9.** (b)	**10.** (c)
11. (d)	**12.** (d)	**13.** (c)	**14.** (b)	**15.** (a)	**16.** (c)	**17.** (d)	**18.** (a)	**19.** (d)	**20.** (d)

Mineral and Energy Resources

A mineral is a natural substance of organic or inorganic origin with definite chemical and physical properties. The mineral resources provide the country with the necessary base for industrial development.

Types of Mineral Resources

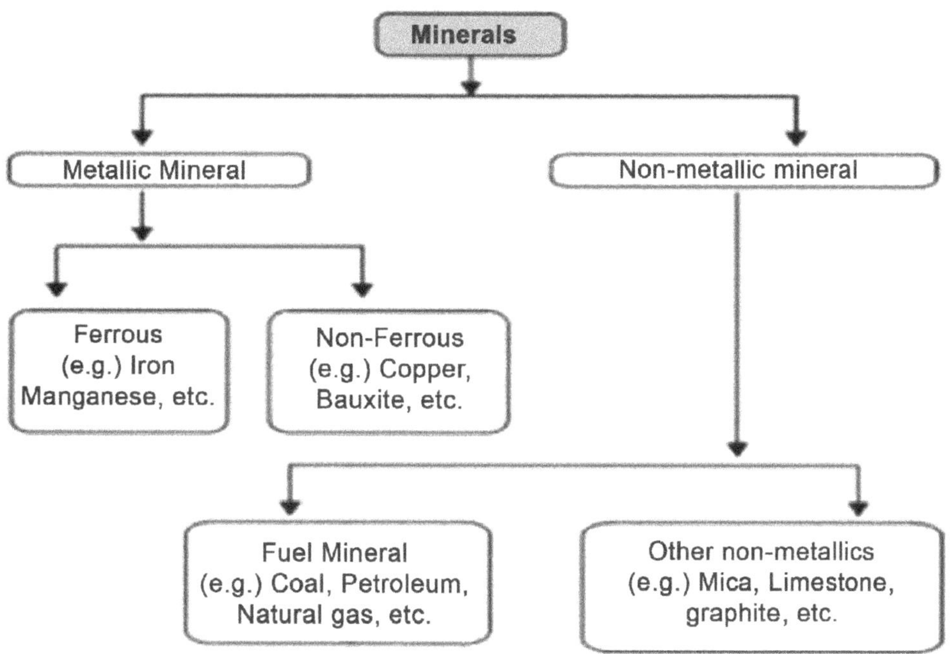

Figure 7.1: Classification of Minerals

Minerals have Certain Characteristics

- These are unevenly distributed over space.
- There is inverse relationship in quality and quantity of minerals i.e. good quality minerals are less in quantity as compared to low quality minerals.
- All minerals are exhaustible over time.

Distribution of Minerals in India

Minerals are generally concentrated in three broad belts in India.

1. **The North-Eastern Plateau Region:** Chhotanagpur (Jharkhand), Odisha Plateau, West Bengal and parts of Chhattisgarh. Iron ore coal, manganese, bauxite, mica.

2. **The South-Western Plateau Region:** Karnataka, Goa and contiguous Tamil Nadu uplands and Kerala. Iron ore, manganese and limestone.

3. **The North-Western Region:** Aravali in Rajasthan and part of Gujarat .Copper, zinc have been major minerals.

   Rajasthan is rich in building stones i.e. sandstone, granite, marble. Gypsum and Fuller's earth deposits are also extensive.

Ferrous Mineral

Iron Ore: India has the largest reserve of iron ore in Asia. The two main types of ore found in our country are haematite and magnetite.

About 95 per cent of total reserves of iron ore is located in the States of Odisha, Jharkhand, Chhattisgarh, Karnataka, Goa, Telangana, Andhra Pradesh and Tamil Nadu.

Orissa Mines: Gurumahisani, Sulaipet, Badampahar (Mayurbhaj), Kiruburu (Kendujhar) and Bonai (Sundergarh).

Jharkhand Mines: Noamundi and Gua are located in Poorbi and Pashchimi Singhbhum districts

Karnataka mines: Ballari district, Baba Budan hills and Kudremukh in Chikkamagaluru district.

Salem and Nilgiris districts of Tamil Nadu are other iron mining regions. Goa has also emerged as an important producer of iron ore.

Manganese: Odisha is the leading producer of Manganese.Iron ore belt -Bonai, Kendujhar, Sundergarh, Gangpur, Koraput, Kalahandi and Bolangir.

Non-Ferrous Minerals:

Bauxite: Odisha happens to be the largest producer of Bauxite. Kalahandi and Sambalpur are the leading producers.

Copper: The Copper deposits mainly occur in Singhbhum district in Jharkhand, Balaghat district in Madhya Pradesh and Jhunjhunu and Alwar districts in Rajasthan.

Non-metallic Minerals

Mica: Mica in India is produced in Jharkhand, Andhra Pradesh, Telanganga and Rajasthan followed by Tamil Nadu, West Bengal and Madhya Pradesh.

Energy Resources

Coal: The most important Gondwana coal fields of India are located in Damodar Valley. They lie in Jharkhand-Bengal coal belt and the mportant coal fields in this region are Raniganj, Jharia, Bokaro, Giridih, Karanpura. Jharia is the largest coal field followed by Raniganj. Tertiary coals occur in Assam, Arunachal Pradesh, Meghalaya and Nagaland.

Petroleum: In Assam, Digboi, Naharkatiya and Moran are important oil producing areas. Mumbai High which lies 160 km off Mumbai was discovered in 1973 and production commenced in 1976.

Natural Gas: Tamil Nadu, Odisha and Andhra Pradesh), Tripura, Rajasthan and off-shore wells in Gujarat and Maharashtra.

Non-Conventional Energy Sources

Nuclear Energy Resources: Uranium deposits occur in the Dharwar rocks. locations along the Singbhum Copper belt. Thorium is mainly obtained from monazite and ilmenite in the beach sands along the coast of Kerala and Tamil Nadu.

Solar Energy: The western part of India has greater potential for the development of solar energy in Gujarat and Rajasthan.

Wind Energy: In Rajasthan, Gujarat, Maharashtra and Karnataka, favourable conditions for wind energy exist.

Tidal and Wave Energy: Large tidal waves are known to occur along the west coast of India. Hence, India has great potential for the development of tidal energy along the coasts but so far these have not yet been utilized.

Geothermal Energy: In India, a geothermal energy plant has been commissioned at Manikaran in Himachal Pradesh.

Bio-energy: It will also process the waste and garbage and produce energy. This will improve economic life of rural areas in developing countries, reduce environmental pollution, enhance self-reliance and reduce pressure on fuel wood. One such project converting municipal waste into energy is Okhla in Delhi.

Exercise

1. Which one of the following is non-ferrous mineral?
   (a) Iron
   (b) Copper
   (c) Manganese
   (d) Mica

2. Which one of the following minerals is not found in the North-Eastern Plateau region?
   (a) Iron ore
   (b) Coal
   (c) Manganese
   (d) Gypsum

3. Which one of the following river valleys coal deposit is not found?
   (a) Damodar
   (b) Sone
   (c) Mahanadi
   (d) Krishna

4. Which of the following minerals are used in Cement Industry?
   (a) Dolomite
   (b) Gypsum
   (c) Copper
   (d) Both (a) and (b)

5. Which one of the following are not the characteristics of mineral?
   (a) Unevenly distributed
   (b) Exhaustible over time.
   (c) High impurities
   (d) Less quantity

6. Which one of the following states has monazite deposit?
   (a) Tamil Nadu
   (b) Kerala
   (c) Maharashtra
   (d) Karnataka

7. Which one of the following minerals is not a building stone?
   (a) Magnesium
   (b) Sandstone
   (c) Granite
   (d) Marble

8. Sundergarh, Mayurbhanj and Jhar places are famous for which of the following minerals?
   (a) Copper
   (b) Uranium
   (c) Coal
   (d) Iron ore

9. Noamundi and Gua are the important iron ore mines located in which of the following states?
   (a) Orissa
   (b) Jharkhand
   (c) Bihar
   (d) West Bengal

10. Which one of the following states is a leading producer of Manganese?
    (a) Jharkhand
    (b) Orissa
    (c) Chhattisgarh
    (d) West Bengal

11. Baba Budan hills and Kudremukh are famous for which mineral in India?
    (a) Copper
    (b) Uranium
    (c) Magnesium
    (d) Iron ore

12. Kalahandi and Sambalpur are the leading producers of which of the following mineral in India?
    (a) Bauxite
    (b) Mica
    (c) Copper
    (d) Coal

13. Which one of the following products is not use copper in manufacturing process?
    (a) Jewelry
    (b) Making wires
    (c) Electric motors
    (d) Aluminium

14. Jharia in Jharkhand is famous for which of the following energy resources?
    (a) Coal
    (b) Petroleum
    (c) Natural gas
    (d) Uranium

15. In which year Mumbai high was discovered?
    (a) 1972
    (b) 1973
    (c) 1974
    (d) 1975

16. In which year Natural Gas Commission was set up?
    (a) 1956
    (b) 1970
    (c) 1961
    (d) 1952

17. Digboi, Naharkatiya and Moran are important oil producing areas located in which state of India?
    (a) Maharashtra
    (b) Assam
    (c) Karnataka
    (d) Rajasthan

18. Which of the following minerals is used in Nuclear energy?
    (a) Uranium
    (b) Thorium
    (c) Mica
    (d) Both (a) and (b)

19. Which of the following is a nuclear power projects in India?
    (a) Tarapur
    (b) Kalpakkam
    (c) Kaiga
    (d) All the above

20. At which one of the following places geothermal energy is commissioned in India?
    (a) Manikaran
    (b) Palakkad
    (c) Kollam
    (d) Udaipur

Answers

1. (b)	**2.** (d)	**3.** (d)	**4.** (d)	**5.** (c)	**6.** (b)	**7.** (a)	**8.** (d)	**9.** (b)	**10.** (b)
11. (d)	**12.** (a)	**13.** (d)	**14.** (a)	**15.** (b)	**16.** (a)	**17.** (b)	**18.** (d)	**19.** (d)	**20.** (a)

Explanations

1. **b** Those which do not have iron content are non-ferrous such as copper, bauxite, etc.

2. **d** It has variety of minerals viz. iron ore coal, manganese, bauxite, mica.

3. **d** Over 97 per cent of coal reserves occur in the valleys of Damodar, Sone, Mahanadi and Godavari.

4. **d** Dolomite and limestone provide raw materials for cement industry.

5. **c** Minerals have certain characteristics. These are unevenly distributed over space. There is inverse relationship in quality and quantity of minerals i.e. good quality minerals are less in quantity as compared to low quality minerals. The third main characteristic is that all minerals are exhaustible over time

6. **b** Kerala has deposits of monazite and thorium, bauxite clay.

7. **a** Rajasthan is rich in building stones i.e. sandstone, granite, marble.

8. **d** In Odisha, iron ore occurs in a series of hill ranges in Sundergarh, Mayurbhanj and Jhar.

9. **b** Jharkhand has some of the oldest iron ore mines and most of the iron and steel plants are located around them. Most of the important mines such as Noamundi and Gua are located in Poorbi and Pashchimi Singhbhum districts.

10. **b** Odisha is the leading producer of Manganese. Major mines in Odisha are located in the central part of the iron ore belt of India, particularly in Bonai, Kendujhar, Sundergarh, Gangpur, Koraput, Kalahandi and Bolangir.

11. **d** In Karnataka, iron ore deposits occur in Sandur - Hospet area of Ballari district, Baba Budan hills and Kudremukh in Chikkamagaluru district and parts of Shivamogga, Chitradurg and Tumakuru districts.

12. **a** Odisha happens to be the largest producer of Bauxite. Kalahandi and Sambalpur are the leading producers. The other two areas which have been increasing their production are Bolangir and Koraput.

13. **d** Copper is an indispensable metal in the electrical industry for making wires, electric motors, transformers and generators. It isalloyable, malleable and ductile. It is also mixed with gold to provide strength to jewellery.

14. **a** Coal lie in Jharkhand-Bengal coal belt and the important coal fields in this region are Raniganj, Jharia, Bokaro, Giridih, Karanpura. Jharia is the largest coal field followed by Raniganj.

15. **b** Mumbai High which lies 160 km off Mumbai was discovered in 1973 and production commenced in 1976.

16. **a** Oil exploration and production was systematically taken up after the Oil and Natural Gas Commission was set up in 1956.

17. **b** In Assam, Digboi, Naharkatiya and Moran are important oil producing areas.

18. **d** Important minerals used for the generation of nuclear energy are uranium and thorium.

19. **d** The important nuclear power projects are Tarapur (Maharashtra), Rawatbhata near Kota (Rajasthan), Kalpakkam (Tamil Nadu), Narora (Uttar Pradesh), Kaiga (Karnataka) and Kakarapara (Gujarat).

20. **a** In India, a geothermal energy plant has been commissioned at Manikaran in Himachal Pradesh.

Manufacturing Industries

Types of Industries

On the basis of size, capital investment and labour force employed, industries are classified as large, medium, small scale, and cottage industries.

On the basis of ownership, industries are categorised as:

(i)   public sector,

(ii) private sector, and

(iii) joint and cooperative sector,

Industries are also classified on the basis of the use of their products such as:

(i)   basic goods industries,

(ii) capital goods industries

(iii) intermediate goods industries, and

(iv) consumer goods industries

Location of Industries

Factors influencing the location of industries are:

Raw Materials: Industries using weight-losing raw materials are located in the regions where raw materials are located. Most of the iron and steel industries are located either near coalfields (Bokaro, Durgapur, etc.) or near sources of iron ore (Bhadravati, Bhilai, and Rourkela).

Power: Power provides the motive force for machines, and therefore, its supply has to be ensured before the location of any industry.

Market

Markets provide the outlets for manufactured products. Heavy machine, machine tools, heavy chemicals are located near the high demand areas as these are market orientated.

Transport: All major industrial plants are located on the trunk rail routes.

Labour

Labour: Industries require skilled labour. In India, labour is quite mobile and is available in large numbers due to our large population.

Major Industries

The Iron and Steel Industry: The other raw materials besides iron ore and coking coal, essential for iron and steel industry are limestone, dolomite, manganese and fire clay.

TISCO: The Tata Iron and Steel plant lies very close to the Mumbai-Kolkata railway line and about 240 km away from Kolkata, which is the nearest port for the export of steel.

IISCO: The Indian Iron and Steel Company (IISCO) set up its first factory at Hirapur and later on another at Kulti. In 1937, the Steel corporation of Bengal was constituted in association with IISCO and set up another iron and steel producing unit at Burnpur (West Bengal).

Visvesvaraiya Iron and Steel Works Ltd. (VISL): The third integrated steel plant, the Visvesvaraiya Iron and Steel Works, initially called the Mysore Iron and Steel Works, is located close to an iron ore producing area of Kemangundi in the Bababudan hills.

Rourkela Steel Plant: The Rourkela Steel plant was set up in 1959 in the Sundargarh district of Odisha in collaboration with Germany.

Bhilai Steel Plant: The Bhilai Steel Plant was established with Russian collaboration in Durg district of Chhattisgarh and started production in 1959.

Durgapur Steel Plant: Durgapur Steel Plant in West Bengal was set up in collaboration with the government of the United Kingdom and started production in 1962.

Bokaro Steel Plant: This steel plant was set up in 1964 at Bokaro with Russian collaboration. This plant was set up on the principle of transportation cost minimisation by creating Bokaro-Rourkela combine.

The Cotton Textile Industry

One, it is a tropical country and cotton is the most comfortable fabric for a hot and humid climate. Second, large quantity of cotton was grown in India. Abundant skilled labour required for this industry was available in this country.

In 1854, the first modern cotton mill was established in Mumbai. It was very close to the cotton producing areas of Gujarat and Maharashtra. Raw cotton used to be brought to Mumbai port to be transported to England.

After Independence, this industry gradually recovered and eventually flourished. Presently, the major centres of the cotton textile industry are Ahmedabad, Bhiwandi, Solapur, Kolhapur, Nagpur, Indore and Ujjain.

Sugar Industry

The sugar industry is the second most important agro-based industry in the country. India is the largest producer of both sugarcane and cane sugar and contributes about 8 per cent of the total sugar production in the world.

Maharashtra has emerged as a leading sugar producer in the country and produces more than one-third of the total production of the sugar in the country.

Uttar Pradesh is the second largest producer of sugar. The sugar factories are concentrated in two belts - the Ganga-Yamuna doab and the tarai region.

Petrochemical Industries

Many items are derived from crude petroleum, which provide raw materials for many new industries, these are collectively known as petrochemical industries. This group of industries is divided into four sub-groups: (i) polymers, (ii) synthetic fibres, (iii) elastomers, and (iv) surfactant intermediate.

Mumbai is the hub of the petrochemical industries. The National Organic Chemicals Industries Limited (NOCIL), established in private sector in 1961, started the first naphtha based chemical industry in Mumbai. Later, several other companies were formed.

Liberalisation, Privatisation, Globalisation (LPG) and Industrial Development in India

The new Industrial Policy was announced in 1991. The industrial licensing system has been abolished for all except six industries related to security, strategic or environmental concerns. At the same time, the number of industries reserved for public sector since 1956 have been reduced from 17 to 4.

Keeping all this in mind, foreign investment has been liberalised and the government has permitted access to an automatic route for Foreign Direct Investment.

The industrial policy has been liberalised to attract private investor both domestic and multi-nationals.

Globalisation means integrating the economy of the country with the world economy. Under this process, goods and services along with capital, labour and resources can move freely from one nation to another.

Industrial Regions in India

Mumbai-Pune Industrial Region: It extends from Mumbai-Thane to Pune and in adjoining districts of Nashik and Solapur. Besides, industrial development has been rapid in Kolaba, Ahmednagar, Satara, Sangli and Jalgaon districts.

Besides, engineering goods, petroleum refining, petrochemicals, leather, synthetic and plastic goods, drugs, fertilisers, electrical, shipbuilding, electronics, software, transport equipment and food industries also developed

Hugli Industrial Region: Located along the Hugli river, this region extends from Bansberia in the north to Birlanagar in the south for a distance of about 100 km. Kolkata-Haora from the nucleus of this industrial region. Historical, geographical, economic and political factors have contributed much to its development.

Kolkata, being the capital city of British India (1773-1911), attracted the British capital. The establishment of first jute mill at Rishra in 1855 ushered in the era of modern industrial clustering in this region.

Bengaluru-Chennai Industrial Region: This region witnessed most rapid industrial growth in post-Independence period. Cotton textile industry was the first to take roots due to the presence of cotton growing areas.

Gujarat Industrial Region: The nucleus of this region lies between Ahmedabad and Vadodara but this region extends upto Valsad and Surat in the south and to Jamnagar in the west

Chotanagpur Region: This region extends over Jharkhand, northern Odisha and western West Bengal and is known for the heavy metallurgical industries. This region owes its development to the discovery of coal in the Damodar Valley and metallic and non-metallic minerals in Jharkhand and northern Odisha.

Vishakhapatnam-Guntur Region: This industrial region extends from Vishakhapatnam district to Kurnool and Prakasam districts in the south. Industrial development of this region hinges upon Vishakhapatnam and Machilipatnam ports and developed agriculture and rich reserves of minerals in their hinterlands. Coalfields of the Godavari basin provide energy.

Gurugram-Delhi-Meerut Region: Industries located in this region have shown very fast growth in the recent past. This region is located far away from the mineral and power resources, and therefore, the industries are light and market-oriented.

Kollam-Thiruvananthapuram Region: This industrial region is spread over Thiruvananthapuram, Kollam, Alwaye, Ernakulam and Alappuzha districts.

Exercise

1. Which of the following are weight -losing raw materials?
   (a) Iron ore   (b) Coal
   (c) Water   (d) Both (a) and (b)

2. Which one of the following Iron and steel industries located near the coalfield?
   (a) Bhadravati   (b) Bhilai
   (c) Rourkela   (d) Bokaro

3. Which one of the following places has not cotton textile industry?
   (a) Mumbai   (b) Ahmedabad
   (c) Surat   (d) Barauni

4. Which one of the following is a pure raw material?
   (a) Copper   (b) Iron ore
   (c) Cotton   (d) Jute

5. Which of the following rivers provide water to the TISCO Plant?
   (a) Subarnarekha   (b) Kharkai
   (c) Damodar   (d) Both (a) and (b)

6. From which of the following mines coal is brought to TISCO
   (a) Joda   (b) Jharia
   (c) Bokaro   (d) Durgapur

7. Which one of the following steel plants receives hydroelectricity from Jog waterfall?
   (a) Visvesvaraiya Iron and Steel Works Ltd
   (b) Indian Iron and Steel Company (IISCO)
   (c) Rourkela Steel Plant
   (d) Bhilai Steel Plant

8. Consider the following steel plants and their location, which one is not correctly matched?
   (a) Rourkela - Bokaro
   (b) Bhilai - Chattisgarh
   (c) Durgapur - West Bengal
   (d) Visvesvaraiya - Mysore

9. In which year Steel Authority of India Limited (SAIL) was created?
   (a) 1970   (b) 1972
   (c) 1975   (d) 1973

10. Bokaro steel plant was set up in collaboration with which Country?
    (a) Germany   (b) Russia
    (c) Britain   (d) US

11. Which of the following steel plants in India was set up during 2nd five year plan?
    (a) Rourkela   (b) Bhilai
    (c) Durgapur   (d) All the above

12. Where the first cotton mill was established in 1854?
    (a) Kolkata   (b) Mumbai
    (c) Chennai   (d) Delhi

13. Which one of the following is the second largest producer of sugar:
    (a) Maharashtra   (b) Punjab
    (c) Uttar Pradesh   (d) Tamil Nadu

14. Which one of the following involved in imparting training in petro-chemical industry?
    (a) Indian Petrochemical Corporation Limited (IPCL)
    (b) Plastic Engineering and Technology (PET)
    (c) Petrofils Cooperative Limited (PCL)
    (d) Central Institute of Plastic Engineering and Technology (CIPET

15. Which one of the following is the largest producer of sugar?
    (a) Uttar Pradesh   (b) Karnataka
    (c) Maharashtra   (d) Bihar

16. In which year Suez Canal was opened?
    (a) 1869   (b) 1902
    (c) 1883   (d) 1879

17. Which one of the following is the reason for slowing down growth of the Hugli Industrial Region?
    (a) Less labor availability
    (b) Drought
    (c) Decline in jute industry
    (d) More Population

18. Which one of the following was capital city of British India?
    (a) Delhi   (b) Mumbai
    (c) Surat   (d) Kolkata

19. Which one of the following is the nucleus of the Hugli Industrial Region?
    (a) Kolkata-Haora   (b) Kolkata-Medinipur
    (c) Kolkata-Rishra   (d) Kolkata-Konnaga

20. Which one of the following region is known for the heavy metallurgical industries?
    (a) Gujarat Industrial Region
    (b) Vishakhapatnam-Guntur Region
    (c) Chotanagpur Region
    (d) Gurugram-Delhi-Meerut Region

Answers

1. (d)   **2.** (d)   **3.** (d)   **4.** (c)   **5.** (d)   **6.** (a)   **7.** (a)   **8.** (a)   **9.** (d)   **10.** (b)

11. (d)   **12.** (b)   **13.** (c)   **14.** (d)   **15.** (c)   **16.** (a)   **17.** (c)   **18.** (d)   **19.** (a)   **20.** (c)

Explanations

1. d In iron and steel industries, iron ore and coal both are weight-losing raw materials.

2. d Most of the iron and steel industries are located either near coalfields (Bokaro, Durgapur, etc.) or near sources of iron ore (Bhadravati, Bhilai, and Rourkela).

3. d Cotton textile industry uses a non-weight-losing raw material and is generally located in large urban centre, e.g. Mumbai, Ahmedabad, Surat, etc

4. c Cotton is a "pure" raw material which does not lose weight in the manufacturing process. so other factors, like, power to drive the looms, labour, capital or market may determine the location of the industry.

5. d The Tata Iron and Steel plant lies very close to the Mumbai-Kolkata railway line and about 240 km away from Kolkata, which is the nearest port for the export of steel. The rivers Subarnarekha and Kharkai provide water to the plant.

6. a The iron ore for the plant is obtained from Noamundi and Badam Pahar and coal is brought from Joda mines in Odisha.

7. a Afterwards, electric furnaces were installed which use hydroelectricity from the Jog Falls hydel power project.

8. a After independence, during the Second Five Year Plan (1956-61), three new integrated steel plants were set up with foreign collaboration: Rourkela in Odisha, Bhilai in Chhattisgarh and Durgapur in West Bengal.

9. d Rourkela in Odisha, Bhilai in Chhattisgarh and Durgapur in West Bengal. These were public sector plants under Hindustan Steel Limited (HSL). In 1973, the Steel Authority of India Limited (SAIL) was created to manage these plants.

10. b Bokaro Steel Plant was set up in 1964 with Russian collaboration.

11. d After independence, during the Second Five Year Plan (1956-61), three new integrated steel plants were set up with foreign collaboration: Rourkela in Odisha, Bhilai in Chhattisgarh and Durgapur in West Bengal.

12. b In 1854, the first modern cotton mill was established in Mumbai.

13. c Uttar Pradesh is the second largest producer of sugar

14. d The Central Institute of Plastic Engineering and Technology (CIPET), involved in imparting training in petro-chemical industry.

15. c Maharashtra has emerged as a leading sugar producer in the country and produces more than one-third of the total production of the sugar in the country.

16. a Mumbai, with cotton hinterland and moist climate favoured the location of cotton textile industry. Opening of the Suez Canal in 1869 provided impetus to the growth of Mumbai port. Machineries were imported through this port.

17. c However, industrial growth of this region has slowed down in comparison to other regions. Decline of the jute industry is one of the reasons.

18. d Kolkata, being the capital city of British India (1773-1911), attracted the British capital.

19. a Kolkata-Haora from the nucleus of this industrial region. Historical, geographical, economic and political factors have contributed much to its development.

20. c This region extends over Jharkhand, northern Odisha and western West Bengal and is known for the heavy metallurgical industries.

Planning and Sustainable Development in Indian Context

Generally, there are two approaches to planning, i.e. sectoral planning and regional planning. Sectoral planning means formulation and implementation of the sets of schemes or programmes aimed at development of various sectors of the economy, such as agriculture, irrigation, manufacturing, power, construction, transport, communication, social infrastructure and services.

Target Area Planning

With the planning experience of about one-and-a-half decades, it was realized that regional imbalances in economic development were getting accentuated.

In the 8th Five Year Plan special area programmes were designed to develop infrastructure in hill areas, north-eastern states, tribal areas and backward areas.

Hill Area Development Programme

Hill Area Development Programmes were initiated during the Fifth Five Year Plan covering 15 districts comprising all the hilly districts of Uttar Pradesh (present Uttarakhand), Mikir Hill and North Cachar hills of Assam, Darjeeling district of West Bengal and Nilgiri district of Tamil Nadu.

Drought Prone Area Programme

This programme was initiated during the Fourth Five Year Plan with the objectives of providing employment to the people in drought-prone areas and creating productive assets. Initially, this programme laid emphasis on the construction of labour-intensive civil works.

The Planning Commission of India (1967) identified 67 districts (entire or partly) of the country prone to drought. The Irrigation Commission (1972) introduced the criterion of 30 per cent irrigated area and demarcated the drought-prone areas.

Sustainable Development

The term development is generally used to describe the state of particular societies and the process of changes experienced by them.

In the post-World War II era, the concept of development was synonymous to economic growth which is measured in terms of temporal increase in gross national product (GNP) and per capita income/per capita consumption.

It reflected the concern of people about undesirable effects of industrial development on the environment. The publication of 'The Population Bomb' by Ehrlich in 1968 and 'The Limits to Growth' by Meadows and others in 1972 further raised the level of fear among environmentalists in particular and people in general. This sets the scenario for the emergence of new models of development under a broad phrase 'sustainable development.'

Measures for Promotion of Sustainable Development

The ecological sustainability of Indira Gandhi Canal Project has been questioned by various scholars. Their point of view has also largely been validated by the course of development this region has taken during the last four decades, which has resulted in degradation of physical environment.

- The first requirement is strict implementation of water management policy.

- In general, the cropping pattern shall not include water intensive crops.

- The CAD programmes such as lining of water courses, land development and levelling and warabandi system (equal distribution of canal water in the command area of outlet) shall be effectively implemented to reduce the conveyance loss of water.

- The areas affected by water logging and soil salinity shall be reclaimed.

- The eco-development through afforestation, shelterbelt plantation and pasture development is necessary particularly in the fragile environment of Stage-II.

- The social sustainability in the region can be achieved only if the land allottees having poor economic background are provided adequate financial and institutional support for cultivation of land.

- The economic sustainability in the region cannot be attained only through development of agriculture and animal husbandry. This shall lead to diversification of economic base and establishment of functional linkages between basic villages, agro-service centres and market centres.

Exercise

1. When the Planning commission was replaced by NITI Aayog?
   (a) 11 January 2019
   (b) 1 January 2005
   (c) 1 January 2015
   (d) 1 January 2020

2. Special area programmes was designed in which of the following five year plan?
   (a) 8th Five Year Plan
   (b) 9th Five Year Plan
   (c) 10th Five Year Plan
   (d) 12th Five Year Plan

3. In which of the following five year plan Hill Area Development Programmes was initiated?
   (a) 9th Five Year Plan
   (b) 5th Five Year Plan
   (c) 6th Five Year Plan
   (d) 10th five year plan

4. Which of the following were the objectives of Drought Prone Area Programme?
   (a) providing employment
   (b) creating productive assets
   (c) Construction of canal
   (d) Both A and B

5. Which of the following are examples of target group programme?
   (a) Hill Area Development Programme.
   (b) The Small Farmers Development Agency (SFDA)
   (c) Marginal Farmers Development Agency (MFDA)
   (d) All the above

6. How many districts of India are prone to draught?
   (a) 70
   (b) 80
   (c) 90
   (d) 67

7. In which year The Population Bomb was published?
   (a) 1968
   (b) 1972
   (c) 1978
   (d) 1960

8. Who among the following is an author of book 'The Limits to Growth'?
   (a) Meadows
   (b) Ehrlich
   (c) Charles Mathew
   (d) Peter vallis

9. Who among the following was headed World Commission on Environment and Development (WCED)?
   (a) Gro Harlem Brundtland
   (b) Donald Brundtland
   (c) Ehrlich Brundtland
   (d) Steve sam Brundtland

10. In which of the following year Indira Gandhi Canal was launched?
    (a) 31 March, 1958
    (b) 31 March, 1959
    (c) 31 March, 1948
    (d) 31 March, 1938

11. What was the total planned length of Indira Gandhi Canal?
    (a) 9060 km
    (b) 1000 Km
    (c) 9900 Km
    (d) 10000 Km

12. Which one of the following is come under the category of backward hill areas?
    (a) Hill areas height above 1200m
    (b) Hill areas height above 900m
    (c) Hill areas height above 600m
    (d) Hill areas height above 1000m

13. ITDP refers to which one of the following?
    (a) Integrated Tourism Development Programme
    (b) Integrated Travel Development Programme
    (c) Integrated Tribal Development Programme
    (d) Integrated Transport Development Programme

14. Which one of the following tribes in India practiced transhumance?
    (a) Gaddis
    (b) Gond
    (c) Bhil
    (d) Santhal

15. Which one of the following is the most crucial factor for sustainable development in Indira Gandhi Canal Command Area?

(a) Agricultural development

(b) Transport development

(c) Colonisation of land

(d) Eco-development

16. Indira Gandhi Canal, previously known as the______________.

(a) Jaislamer canal

(b) Gujrat canal

(c) Punjab canal

(d) Rajasthan canal

17. Which of the following crops were introduced after the construction of Indira Gandhi canal?

(a) Wheat

(b) Cotton

(c) Groundnut

(d) All the above

18. Which of the following are drawbacks of canal irrigation?

(a) Waterlogging

(b) Soil salinity

(c) Large yield

(d) Both (a) and (b)

19. Equal distribution of canal water in the command area of outlet is called ______?

(a) Chakbandi

(b) Land fertility

(c) Warbandi

(d) Dhakbandi

20. In which year Gaddis were included among 'scheduled tribes'?

(a) 1970s

(b) 1980s

(c) 1990

(d) 1960

Answers

1. (c)	**2.** (a)	**3.** (b)	**4.** (d)	**5.** (d)	**6.** (d)	**7.** (a)	**8.** (a)	**9.** (a)	**10.** (a)
11. (a)	**12.** (c)	**13.** (c)	**14.** (a)	**15.** (d)	**16.** (d)	**17.** (d)	**18.** (d)	**19.** (c)	**20.** (a)

Explanations

1. **c** On 1 January 2015, the NITI Aayog was formed. India adopted centralised planning after Independence, but subsequently, it graduated into decentralised multi-level planning.

2. **a** In the 8th Five Year Plan special area programmes were designed to develop infrastructure in hill areas, north-eastern states, tribal areas and backward areas.

3. **b**

4. **d** Drought Prone Area Programme was initiated during the Fourth Five Year Plan with the objectives of providing employment to the people in drought-prone areas and creating productive assets.

5. **d** Some of the examples of programmes directed towards the development of target areas are Command Area Development Programme, Drought Prone Area Development Programme, Desert Development Programme, Hill Area Development Programme. The Small Farmers Development Agency (SFDA) and Marginal Farmers Development Agency (MFDA) which are the examples of target group programme.

6. **d** The Planning Commission of India (1967) identified 67 districts (entire or partly) of the country prone to drought.

7. **a** The publication of 'The Population Bomb' by Ehrlich in 1968.

8. **a** The Limits to Growth' by Meadows and others in 1972 further raised the level of fear among environmentalists in particular and people in general.

9. **a** The United Nations established a World Commission on Environment and Development (WCED) headed by the Norwegian Prime Minister Gro Harlem Brundtland. The Commission gave its report (also known as Brundtland Report) entitled 'Our Common Future' in 1987.

10. **a** Indira Gandhi Canal, previously known as the Rajasthan Canal, is one of the largest canal systems in India. Conceived by Kanwar Sain in 1948, the canal project was launched on 31 March, 1958.

11. **a** The canal originates at Harike barrage in Punjab and runs parallel to Pakistan border at an average distance of 40 km in Thar Desert (Marusthali) of Rajasthan. The total planned length of the system is 9,060 km catering to the irrigation needs of a total culturable command area of 19.63 lakh hectares.

12. **c** The National Committee on the Development of Backward Area in 1981 recommended that all the hill areas in the country having height above 600 m and not covered under tribal sub-plan be treated as backward hill areas.

13. **c** Under Fig. 9.1 * The name Bharmaur is derived from Sanskrit word Brahmaur. In this book Bharmaur has been used to retain the colloquial flavour. the Fifth Five Year Plan, the tribal sub-plan was introduced in 1974 and Bharmaur was designated as one of the five Integrated Tribal Development Projects (ITDP) in Himachal Pradesh.

14. **a** Bharmaur is inhabited by 'Gaddi', a tribal community who have maintained a distinct identity in the Himalayan region as they practised transhumance and conversed through Gaddiali dialect.

15. **d** The ecological sustainability of Indira Gandhi Canal Project has been questioned by various scholars.

16. **d** Indira Gandhi Canal, previously known as the Rajasthan Canal, is one of the largest canal systems in India.

17. **d** Soil moisture has been a limiting factor in successful growing of crops in this area. Spread of canal irrigation has led to increase in cultivated area and intensity of cropping. The traditional crops sown in the area, gram, bajra and jowar have been replaced by wheat, cotton, groundnut and rice.

18. **d** This has also caused waterlogging Fig. 9.4: Indira Gandhi Canal Fig. 9.5 : Indira Gandhi Canal and its adjoining areas and soil salinity, and thus, in the long run, it hampers the sustainability of agriculture

19. **c** Warabandi system - equal distribution of canal water in the command area of outlet

20. **a** The process of development of tribal area of Bharmaur started in 1970s when Gaddis were included among 'scheduled tribes'.

CHAPTER 10

Transport and Communication

The use of transport and communication depends upon our need to move things from place of their availability to the place of their use.

Land Transport: The pathways and unmetalled roads have been used for transportation in India since ancient times.

Road Transport

India has one of the second largest road networks in the world with a total length of about 56 lakh km (morth.nic.in, Annual Report 2017-18).

The first serious attempt was made in 1943 when 'Nagpur Plan' was drawn.

National Highways: The main roads which are constructed and maintained by the Central Government are known as the National Highways. These roads are meant for inter-state transport and movement of defence men and material in strategic areas. The length of the National Highways has increased from 19,700 km in 1951 to 101011 km in 2016. The National Highways constitute only about 2 per cent of the total road length but carry 40 per cent of the road traffic.

The National Highways Authority of India (NHAI) was operationalised in 1995. It is an autonomous body under the Ministry of Surface Transport.

State Highways

These are constructed and maintained by state governments. They join the state capitals with district headquarters and other important towns. These constitute 4 per cent of total road length in the country.

District Roads

These roads are the connecting link between District Headquarters and the other important nodes in the district. They account for 14 per cent of the total road length of the country.

Rural Roads

These roads are vital for providing links in the rural areas. About 80 per cent of the total road length in India are categorised as rural roads.

Other Roads

The Border Road Organization (BRO) was established in May 1960 for accelerating economic development and strengthening defense preparedness through rapid and coordinated improvement of strategically important roads along the northern and north-eastern boundary of the country.

Rail Transport

Indian Railway was introduced in 1853, when a line was constructed from Bombay to Thane covering a distance of 34 km.

Indian Railways is the largest government undertaking in the country. The length of Indian Railways network was 66,030 km as on 31 March 2015.

Metro rail has revolutionlised the urban transport system in Kolkata and Delhi. replacement of diesel buses by CNG-run vehicles along with the introduction of metro is a welcome step towards controlling the air pollution in urban centres.

Water Transport

Waterways is an important mode of transport for both passenger and cargo traffic in India. The water transport is of two types– (a) inland waterways, and (b) oceanic waterways.

Inland Waterways

It was the chief mode of transport before the advent of railways. India has 14,500 km of navigable waterways, contributing about 1% to the country's transportation. For the development, maintenance and regulation of national waterways in the country, the Inland Waterways Authority was set up in 1986.

Waterways	Stretch	Specification
NW 1	Allahabad-Haldia stretch (1,620 km)	It is one of the most important waterways in India, which is navigable by mechanical boats up to Patna and by ordinary boats up to Haridwar. It is divided into three parts for developmental purposes - (i) Haldia-Farakka (560 km), (ii) Farakka-Patna (460 km), (iii) Patna-Allahabad (600 km).)
NW 2	Sadiya-Dhubri Stretch (891 km)	Brahmaputra is navigable by streamers up to Dibrugarh (1,384 km) which is shared by India and Bangladesh
NW 3	Kottapuram-Kollam Stretch (205 km)	It includes 168 km of west coast along with Champakara canal (14 km) and Udyogmandal canal (23 km).
NW 4	Specified streches of Godavari and Krishna rivers along with Kakinada Puducherry stretch of canals (1078 km)	
NW 5	Specified of river Brahmani with Matai river, delta channels of Mahanadi and Brahmani rivers and East Coast canals (588 km).	

Oceanic Routes

Oceanic routes play an important role in the transport sector of India's economy. Approximately 95 per cent of India's foreign trade by volume and 70 per cent by value moves through ocean routes.

Air Transportation

Air transport in India made a beginning in 1911 when airmail operation commenced over a little distance of 10 km between Allahabad and Naini. Pawan Hans is the helicopter service operating in hilly areas and is widely used by tourists in north-eastern sector.

Oil and Gas Pipelines

Oil India Limited (OIL) under the administrative set up of the Ministry of Petroleum and Natural Gas is engaged in the exploration, production and transportation of crude oil and natural gas. It was incorporated in 1959 as a company. Asia's first cross country pipeline covering a distance of 1,157 km was constructed by OIL from Naharkatiya oilfield in Assam to Barauni refinery in Bihar.

Another extensive network of pipelines has been constructed in the western region of India of which Ankleshwar-Koyali, Mumbai HighKoyali and Hazira-Vijaipur-Jagdishpur (HVJ) are most important.

Communication Networks

Initially, the means of communication were also the means of transportation. Invention of postoffice, telegraph, printing press, telephone, satellite, etc has made the communication much faster and easier.

Mass Communication System

Radio

Radio broadcasting started in India in 1923 by the Radio Club of Bombay. Government took this opportunity and brought this popular mode of communication under its control in 1930 under the Indian Broadcasting System. It was changed to All India Radio in 1936 and to Akashwani in 1957.

Television (T.V.)

After 1972, several other centres became operational. In 1976, TV was delinked from All India Radio (AIR) and got a separate identity as Doordarshan (DD). After INSAT-IA (National Television-DD1) became operational, Common National Programmes (CNP) were started for the entire network and its services were extended to the backward and remote rural areas.

Satellite Communication

On the basis of configuration and purposes, satellite system in India can be grouped into two: Indian National Satellite System (INSAT) and Indian Remote Sensing Satellite System (IRS).

The IRS satellite system became operational with the launching of IRS-IA in March 1988 from Vaikanour in Russia. The National Remote Sensing Centre (NRSC) at Hyderabad provides facilities for acquisition of data and its processing.

Exercise

1. What is the rank of India in terms road networks in world?
   - (a) First
   - (b) Second
   - (c) Third
   - (d) Fourth

2. The Grand Trunk (GT) road connecting which two places in India?
   - (a) Calcutta to Peshawar
   - (b) Delhi to Bombay
   - (c) Calcutta to Chennai
   - (d) Calcutta to Patna

3. Nagpur Plan was associated with which of the following transport network in India?
   - (a) Railway
   - (b) Airway
   - (c) Inland waterway
   - (d) Road

4. Which of the following plan was introduced to improve the conditions of roads in India?
   - (a) twenty-year road plan (1961)
   - (b) Nehru Plan
   - (c) Nagpur Plan
   - (d) Road plan

5. What percent of Passenger in India carried by roads every year?
   - (a) 85 per cent of passenger
   - (b) 35 per cent of passenger
   - (c) 15 per cent of passenger
   - (d) 95 per cent of passenger

6. When National Highways Authority of India (NHAI) was operationalized?
   - (a) 1996
   - (b) 1990
   - (c) 1998
   - (d) 1995

7. What is the present length of National Highway in India?
   - (a) 101011 km
   - (b) 191011 km
   - (c) 211011 km
   - (d) 981011 km

8. What is the total length of Golden Quadrilateral?
   - (a) 2,846-km long
   - (b) 3,846-km long
   - (c) 5,846-km long
   - (d) 5,006-km long

9. Which of the two places in India is connected by East- West corridor?
   - (a) Silchar to Porbander
   - (b) Silchar to Mumbai
   - (c) Silchar to surat
   - (d) Silchar to Bikaner

10. Which of the following types of road in India has maximum percentage coverage?
    - (a) National highway
    - (b) State highway
    - (c) Rural roads
    - (d) Border road

11. Which two places are connecting by Konkan railway?
    - (a) Roha to Manglore
    - (b) Goa to Mumbai
    - (c) Chennai to Manglore
    - (d) Banglore to manglore

12. Which one of the following states is not a partner of Konkan railway?
    - (a) Maharashtra
    - (b) Goa
    - (c) Karnataka
    - (d) Kerala

13. In how many zones Indian railway is divided?
    - (a) 18 zones
    - (b) 16 zones
    - (c) 20 zones
    - (d) 10 zones

14. What is the target year for the completion of Bharatmala project?
    - (a) 2020
    - (b) 2021
    - (c) 2022
    - (d) 2019

15. What is the Headqurter of Southeastern railway zone?
    - (a) Kolkata
    - (b) Chennai
    - (c) Secunderabad
    - (d) Coimbtore

16. In which year Inland waterways authority was set-up?
    - (a) 1986
    - (b) 1990
    - (c) 1994
    - (d) 1995

17. Which one of the following Inland waterways is connecting Kottapuram to Kollam?
    - (a) NW1
    - (b) NW2
    - (c) NW5
    - (d) NW3

18. What percent of India's foreign trade moves through ocean routes?
    - (a) 95 per cent
    - (b) 80 per cent
    - (c) 70 per cent
    - (d) 65 per cent

19. In which year air transport in India began?
    - (a) 1912
    - (b) 1911
    - (c) 1916
    - (d) 1919

20. In which of the following year air transport was nationalized ?
    - (a) 1951
    - (b) 1954
    - (c) 1953
    - (d) 1960

Answers

1. (b)   **2.** (a)   **3.** (d)   **4.** (a)   **5.** (a)   **6.** (d)   **7.** (a)   **8.** (c)   **9.** (a)   **10.** (c)

11. (a)   **12.** (d)   **13.** (b)   **14.** (c)   **15.** (a)   **16.** (a)   **17.** (d)   **18.** (a)   **19.** (b)   **20.** (c)

Explanations

1. **b** India has one of the second largest road networks in the world with a total length of about 56 lakh km (morth.nic.in, Annual Report 2017-18).

2. **a** Sher Shah Suri built the Shahi (Royal) (Royal) road to strengthen and consolidate his empire from the Indus Valley to the Sonar Valley in Bengal. This road was renamed the Grand Trunk (GT) road during the British period, connecting Calcutta and Peshawar.

3. **d** Road transport in modern sense was very limited in India before World War-II. The first serious attempt was made in 1943 when 'Nagpur Plan' was drawn.

4. **a** After Independence, twenty-year road plan (1961) was introduced to improve the conditions of roads in India.

5. **a** About 85 per cent of passenger and 70 per cent of freight traffic are carried by roads every year.

6. **d** The National Highways Authority of India (NHAI) was operationalised in 1995.

7. **a** The length of the National Highways has increased from 19,700 km in 1951 to 101011 km in 2016.

8. **c** It comprises construction of 5,846-km long 4/6 lane, high density traffic corridor, to connect India's four big metro cities of Delhi-Mumbai-ChennaiKolkata.

9. **a** The East-West Corridor has been planned to connect Silchar in Assam with the port town of Porbandar in Gujarat with 3,640-km of road length.

10. **c** About 80 per cent of the total road length in India are categorised as rural roads.

11. **a** One of the important achievements of the Indian Railways has been the construction of Konkan Railway in 1998. It is 760-km long rail route connecting Roha in Maharashtra to Mangalore in Karnataka.

12. **d** The states of Maharashtra, Goa and Karnataka are partners in this undertaking.

13. **b** Thus, in India, the railway system has been divided into 16 zones.

14. **c** Bharatmalaprogramme is targeted for completion by 2022.

15. **a**

16. **a** For the development, maintenance and regulation of national waterways in the country, the Inland Waterways Authority was set up in 1986.

17. **d** NW 3 Kottapuram-Kollam stretch (205 km)

18. **a** Approximately 95 per cent of India's foreign trade by volume and 70 per cent by value moves through ocean routes.

19. **b** Air transport in India made a beginning in 1911 when airmail operation commenced over a little distance of 10 km between Allahabad and Naini.

20. **c** 1953 – Air transport was nationalised and two Corporations, Air India International and Indian Airlines were formed.

CHAPTER 11

International Trade

The composition of commodities in India's international trade has been undergoing a change over the years

The shares of ore minerals and manufactured goods have largely remained constant over the years from 2009-10 to 2010-11and 2015-16 to 2016-17.

The decline in traditional items is largely due to the tough international competition. Amongst the agricultural products, there is a decline in the export of traditional items, such as coffee, cashew, etc., though an increase has been registered in floricultural products, fresh fruits, marine products and sugar, etc.

Changing Patterns of the Composition of India's Import

India faced serious food shortage during 1950s and 1960s. The major item of import at that time was foodgrain, capital goods, machinery and equipment.

Import of food and allied products declined with a fall in imports of edible oils. Other major items of India's import include pearls and semi-precious stones, gold and silver, metalliferrous ores and metal scrap, non-ferrous metals, electronic goods, etc.

Direction of Trade

India has trade relations with most of the countries and major trading blocks of the world.

India aims to double its share in the international trade within the next five years. It has already started adopting suitable measures such as import liberalisation, reduction in import duties, delicensing and change from process to product patents.

Seaports of India

India is surrounded by sea from three sides and is bestowed with a long coastline.

Some of the Indian ports along with their hinterlands are as follows :

Kandla Port

Situated at the head of Gulf of Kuchchh has been developed as a major port to cater to the needs of western and north western parts of the country and also to reduce the pressure at Mumbai port.

Mumbai is a natural harbour and the biggest port of the country. The port is situated closer to the general routes from the countries of Middle East, Mediterranean countries, North Africa, North America and Europe where the major share of country's overseas trade is carried out.

Jawaharlal Nehru Port at NhavaSheva was developed as a satellite port to relieve the pressure at the Mumbai port. It is the largest container port in India

Marmagao Port, situated at the entrance of the Zuari estuary, is a natural harbour in Goa. It gained significance after its remodelling in 1961 to handle iron-ore exports to Japan.

New Mangalore Port is located in the state of Karnataka and caters to the needs of the export of iron-ore and iron-concentrates.

Kochchi Port, situated at the head of VembanadKayal, popularly known as the 'Queen of the Arabian Sea', is also a natural harbour.

Kolkata Port is located on the Hugli river, 128 km inland from the Bay of Bengal. Like the Mumbai port, this port was also developed by the British. Kolkata had the initial advantage of being the capital of British India.

Haldia Port is located 105 km downstream from Kolkata. It has been constructed to reduce the congestion at Kolkata port.

Paradwip Port is situated in the Mahanadi delta, about 100 km from Cuttack. It has the deepest harbourspecially suited to handle very large vessels.

Visakhapatnam Port in Andhra Pradesh is a land-locked harbour, connected to the sea by a channel cut through solid rock and sand.

Chennai Port is one of the oldest ports on the eastern coast. It is an artificial harbour built in 1859. It is not much suitable for large ships because of the shallow waters near the coast

Ennore, a newly developed port in Tamil Nadu, has been constructed 25 km north of Chennai to relieve the pressure at Chennai port.

Tuticorin Port was also developed to relieve the pressure of Chennai port. It deals with a variety of cargo, including coal, salt, food grains, edible oils, sugar, chemicals and petroleum products

Airports

Air transport plays an important role in the international trade.There were 25 major airports functioning in the country (Annual Report 2016-17).

Exercise

1. Trade between two countries is termed as -
   - (a) Internal trade
   - (b) External trade
   - (c) International trade
   - (d) Local trade

2. Which one of the following is a land locked harbour?
   - (a) Vishakhapatnam
   - (b) Mumbai
   - (c) Ennor
   - (d) Haldia

3. Most of India's foreign trade is carried through –
   - (a) Land and sea
   - (b) Land and air
   - (c) Sea and air
   - (d) Sea

4. International Trade is ______ beneficial as no country is self-sufficient.
   - (a) Similarly
   - (b) Mutually
   - (c) Both
   - (d) Neither

5. What percent is the India's contribution in international trade?
   - (a) Ten
   - (b) One
   - (c) Five
   - (d) Three

6. India faced serious food shortage during which of the following decade?
   - (a) 1940s and 1960s.
   - (b) 1950s and 1970s.
   - (c) 1940s and 1950s.
   - (d) 1950s and 1960s.

7. At present, India has ______ major ports.
   - (a) 10
   - (b) 11
   - (c) 12
   - (d) 13

8. Karachi port is located in which of the following country?
   - (a) Pakistan
   - (b) Bangladesh
   - (c) India
   - (d) Nepal

9. Chittagong port is located in which of the following country?
   - (a) India
   - (b) Pakistan
   - (c) Bangladesh
   - (d) Bhutan

10. Diamond Harbour near Kolkata is on which of the following river?
    - (a) Ganga
    - (b) Yamuna
    - (c) Mahanadi
    - (d) Hugli

11. Which of the following port is not located on the eastern side of the country?
    - (a) Kandla
    - (b) Marmagao
    - (c) Mumbai
    - (d) Haldia

12. Which of the following state has the highest number of the ports?
    - (a) Maharashtra
    - (b) Orissa
    - (c) Tamil Nadu
    - (d) Kerala

13. There were ______ major airports functioning in the country (Annual Report 2016-17).
    - (a) 25
    - (b) 20
    - (c) 15
    - (d) 30

14. Ennore port is located in which of the following state?
    - (a) Kerala
    - (b) Orissa
    - (c) Tamil Nadu
    - (d) West Bengal

15. ______ Port, situated at the head of VembanadKayal, popularly known as the 'Queen of the Arabian Sea', is also a natural harbour.
    - (a) Kandla
    - (b) Ennore
    - (c) Marmagaon
    - (d) Kochchi

16. Which of the following port has the country's largest oil terminal?
    - (a) Mumbai
    - (b) Marmagaon
    - (c) New Manglore
    - (d) Kandla

17. Consider the following statements:
    1. India is surrounded by sea from three sides and is bestowed with a long coastline.
    2. India is that its east coast has more ports than its west coast.

    Which of the statements given above is/are NOT correct?
    - (a) 1 only
    - (b) 2 only
    - (c) Both 1 and 2
    - (d) Neither 1 nor 2

18. Assertion: The share of agriculture and allied products has declined, whereas, shares of petroleum and crude products and other commodities have increased.

    Reason: The decline in traditional items is largely due to the tough international competition.

    - (a) Both the Assertion and the Reason are correct and the Reason is the correct explanation of Assertion.
    - (b) Both the Assertion and the Reason are correct but the Reason is not the correct explanation of Assertion.
    - (c) The Assertion isincorrect but the Reason is correct.
    - (d) The Assertion is correct but the Reason is incorrect.

19. Consider the following statements:

1. The nature of India's foreign trade has changed over the years.
2. Though there has been an increase in the total volume of import and export, the value of export continued to be higher than that of imports.

Which of the statements given above is/are correct?

(a) 1 only

(b) 2 only

(c) Both 1 and 2

(d) Neither 1 nor 2

20. Which of the following are the reasons for the sharp rise in India's international trade?

1. Rise in the manufacturing sectors
2. Liberal policies of the government
3. Diversification of markets

Select the correct answer using the code given below:

(a) 1 and 2 only

(b) 2 and 3 only

(c) 1 and 3 only

(d) 1, 2 and 3

Answers

1. (c)	2. (a)	3. (c)	4. (b)	5. (b)	6. (d)	7. (c)	8. (a)	9. (c)	10. (d)
11. (d)	12. (c)	13. (a)	14. (c)	15. (d)	16. (a)	17. (b)	18. (a)	19. (a)	20. (d)

Explanations

1. **c** Trade between two countries is termed as International Trade.

2. **a** Visakhapatnam Port in Andhra Pradesh is a land-locked harbour, connected to the sea by a channel cut through solid rock and sand.

3. **c** Most of India's foreign trade is carried through sea and air routes. However, a small portion is also carried through land route to neighbouring countries like Nepal, Bhutan, Bangladesh and Pakistan.

4. **b** International Trade is mutually beneficial as no country is self-sufficient.

5. **b** Although India's contribution in the world trade is as low as one per cent of the total volume, yet it plays a significant role in the world economy.

6. **d** India faced serious food shortage during 1950s and 1960s. The major item of import at that time was foodgrain, capital goods, machinery and equipment.

7. **c** At present, India has 12 major ports and 200 minor or intermediate ports.

8. **a** Karachi port is located in Pakistan.

9. **c** Chittagong port was located inerstwhile east-Pakistan and now in Bangladesh.

10. **d** Diamond Harbour near Kolkata is on river Hugli in the east.

11. **d** Haldia Port is located 105 km downstream from Kolkata.

12. **c** Tamil Nadu has the highest number of ports.

13. **a** There were 25 major airports functioning in the country (Annual Report 2016-17).

14. **c** Ennore, a newly developed port in Tamil Nadu, has been constructed 25 km north of Chennai to relieve the pressure at Chennai port.

15. **d** Kochchi Port, situated at the head of VembanadKayal, popularly known as the 'Queen of the Arabian Sea', is also a natural harbour. This port has an advantageous location being close to the Suez-Colombo route. It caters to the needs of Kerala, southernKarnataka and south western Tamil Nadu.

16. **a** Mumbai is a natural harbour and the biggest port of the country. The port is situated closer to the general routes from the countries of Middle East, Mediterranean countries, North Africa, North America and Europe where the major share of country's overseas trade is carried out. The port is 20 km long and 6-10 km wide with 54 berths and has the country's largest oil terminal. M.P., Maharashtra, Gujarat, U.P. and parts of Rajasthan constitute the main hinterlands of Mumbai ports.

17. **b** India is surrounded by sea from three sides and is bestowed with a long coastline.India is that its west coast has more ports than its east coast.

18. **a** The share of agriculture and allied products has declined, whereas, shares of petroleum and crude products and other commodities have increased.The decline in traditional items is largely due to the tough international competition.

19. **a** The nature of India's foreign trade has changed over the years. Though there has been an increase in the total volume of import and export, the value of import continued to be higher than that of exports.

20. **d** There are numerous reasons for this sharp rise in overseas trade, such as the momentum picked up by the manufacturing sectors, the liberal policies of the government and the diversification of markets.

CHAPTER 12

Geographical Perspective on Selected Issues and Problems

Environmental Pollution

Environmental pollution results from 'the release of substances and energy from waste products of human activities.

Water Pollution

Indiscriminate use of water by increasing population and industrial expansion has led degradation of the quality of water considerably. Surface water available from rivers, canals, lakes, etc. is never pure.

Though water pollutants are also created from natural sources (erosion, landslides, decay and decomposition of plants and animals, etc.) pollutants from human activities are the real causes of concern. Human beings pollute the water through industrial, agricultural and cultural activities. Among these activities, industry is the most significant contributor.

Water pollution is a source of various water- borne diseases. The diseases commonly caused due to contaminated water are diarrhoea, intestinal worms, hepatitis, etc. The World Health Organization shows that about one-fourth of the communicable diseases in India are water-borne.

Namami Gange Programme

Ganga, as a river, has national importance but the river requires cleaning by effectively controlling the pollution for its water.

The Union Government has launched the 'Namami Gange Programme' with the following objectives:

- developing sewerage treatment systems in towns,

- monitoring of industrial effluents,

- development of river front,

- afforestation along the bank of increase biodiversity,

- cleaning of the river surface,

- development of 'Ganga Grams' in Uttarakhand, UP, Bihar, Jharkhand and West Bengal, and

- creating public awareness to avoid adding pollutants in to the river even in the form of rituals.

Air Pollution

Air pollution is taken as addition of contaminants, like dust, fumes, gas, fog, odour, smoke or vapour to the air in substantial proportion and duration that may be harmful to flora and fauna and to property.

Smoky fog over cities called as urban smog is caused by atmospheric pollution.

Noise Pollution

Noise pollution refers to the state of unbearable and uncomfortable to human beings which is caused by noise from different sources. This matter has become a serious concern only in recent years due to a variety of technological innovations.

The main sources of noise pollution are various factories, mechanised construction and demolition works, automobiles and aircraft, etc.

Of all these sources, the biggest nuisance is the noise produced by traffic, because its intensity and nature depend upon factors, such as the type of aircraft, vehicle, train and the condition of road, as well as, that of vehicle (in case of automobiles)

Urban Waste Disposal

Urban areas are generally marked by overcrowding, congestion, inadequate facilities to support the fast growing population and consequent poor sanitary conditions and foul air. Environmental pollution by solid wastes has now got significance because of enormous growth in the quantity of wastes generated from various sources.

Solid wastes cause health hazard through creation of obnoxious smell, and harbouring of flies and rodents, which act as carriers of diseases like typhoid, diphtheria, diarrhoea, malaria and cholera, etc.

Urban waste disposal is a serious problem in India. In metropolitan cities like Mumbai, Kolkata, Chennai, Bengaluru, etc., about 90 per cent of the solid waste is collected and disposed.

Rural-Urban Migration

In developing countries, poor, semi-illiterate and the unskilled like Ramesh migrating from rural areas frequently end up performing menial jobs at low wages in informal sector in urban areas. Since wages are very low to support the family at the place of destination, the spouses are left behind in rural areas to look after children and elderly people.

Land Degradation

The pressure on agricultural land increases not only due to the limited availability but also by deterioration of quality of agricultural land. Soil erosion, waterlogging, salinisation and alkalinisation of land lead to land degradation.

Exercise

1. There are many types of pollution. They are classified on the basis of ___________ through which pollutants are transported and diffused.
   (a) Medium   (b) Speed
   (c) Region   (d) Space

2. Which one of the following river is highly polluted?
   (a) Brahmaputra   (b) Sutlej
   (c) Yamuna   (d) Godavari

3. Which one of the following disease is caused by water pollution?
   (a) Conjunctivitis
   (b) Diarrhorea
   (c) Respiratory infections
   (d) Bronchitis

4. Which one of the following is the cause of acid rain?
   (a) Water pollution   (b) Land pollution
   (c) Noise pollution   (d) Air pollution

5. Push and pull factors are responsible for–
   (a) Migration   (b) Land degradation
   (c) Slums   (d) Air pollution

6. Which one of the following is not a source of noise pollution?
   (a) Factories
   (b) Mechanised construction
   (c) Automobiles
   (d) Carbon dioxide

7. Which one of the following cities release domestic waste into the river?
   (a) Kanpur   (b) Allahabad
   (c) Varanasi   (d) All the above

8. Which one of the following is responsible for increase in the nitrate content in water?
   (a) Fertilizer   (b) Crop residue
   (c) Salt   (d) Cow dung

9. Smog is caused by which of the following pollution?
   (a) Soil pollution   (b) Water pollution
   (c) Air pollution   (d) Noise pollution

10. In which of the following places in India have largest concentration of Bhils?
    (a) Jhabua   (b) West singhbhum
    (c) Raipur   (d) Alwar

11. Which of the following ministries funded watershed management plan?
    (a) Rural Development   (b) Agriculture
    (c) Urban   (d) Both (a) and (b)

12. Which one of the following is not a socio-environmental hazard?
    (a) Open defecation
    (b) unregulated drainage system
    (c) overcrowded narrow street patterns
    (d) Park

13. Which one of the following is an example of solid waste?
    (a) small pieces of metals
    (b) polythene bags
    (c) broken glassware
    (d) All the above

14. Which of the following diseases caused by solid waste?
    (a) Typhoid   (b) Diptheria
    (c) Malaria   (d) All the above

15. Which of the following are features of slum areas?
    (a) poor ventilation   (b) lack of basic amenities
    (c) dilapidated houses   (d) All the above

16. What percent of population migrated to rural to urban population?
    (a) 29 per cent   (b) 99 per cent
    (c) 59 per cent   (d) 89 per cent

17. How much of world's population will live in urban areas by 2050?
    (a) two-thirds   (b) two-fourth
    (c) three-fourth   (d) one-half

18. What are different types of diseases occurred due to air pollution?
    (a) Respiratory   (b) nervous
    (c) circulatory systems (d) All the above

19. In which of the following states 'Ganga gram' developed?
    (a) Uttarakhand   (b) UP
    (c) Bihar   (d) All the above

20. Which of the following land degradation is caused by human action?
    (a) degraded forests   (b) shifting cultivation
    (c) Mining   (d) All the above

Answers

1. (a)   **2.** (c)   **3.** (b)   **4.** (d)   **5.** (a)   **6.** (d)   **7.** (d)   **8.** (a)   **9.** (c)   **10.** (a)

11. (d)   **12.** (d)   **13.** (d)   **14.** (d)   **15.** (d)   **16.** (a)   **17.** (a)   **18.** (d)   **19.** (d)   **20.** (d)

Explanations

1. a There are many types of pollution. They are classified on the basis of medium through which pollutants are transported and diffused.

2. c Yamuna is the most polluted river.

3. b Diarrhorea is caused by water pollution.

4. d Air pollution is the cause of acid rain.

5. a Push and pull factors are responsible for migration.

6. d The main sources of noise pollution are various factories, mechanised construction and demolition works, automobiles and aircraft, etc.

7. d Cities of Kanpur, Allahabad, Varanasi, Patna and Kolkata release domestic waste into the river

8. a Fertiliser induces an increase in the nitrate content of surface waters.

9. c Smoky fog over cities called as urban smog is caused by atmospheric pollution. It proves very harmful to human health.

10. a Jhabua district is located in the westernmost agro-climatic zone in Madhya Pradesh. It is, in fact, one of the five most backward districts of the country. It is characterised by high concentration of tribal population (mostly Bhils).

11. d The watershed management programmes funded by both the ministries of "Rural Development" and "Agriculture", Government of India, have been successfully implemented in Jhabua district which has gone a long way in preventing land degradation and improving soil quality.

12. d Open defecation, unregulated drainage system and overcrowded narrow street patterns are serious health and socioenvironmental hazards.

13. d Solid waste refers to a variety of old and used articles, for example stained small pieces of metals, broken glassware, plastic containers, polythene bags, ash, floppies, CDs, etc., dumped at different places.

14. d Solid wastes cause health hazard through creation of obnoxious smell, and harbouring of flies and rodents, which act as carriers of diseases like typhoid, diphtheria, diarrhoea, malaria and cholera, etc.

15. d Slums are residential areas of the least choice, dilapidated houses, poor hygienic conditions, poor ventilation, lack of basic amenities, like drinking water, light and toilet facilities, etc.

16. a In India, it is estimated that after 1961 around 60 per cent of the urban growth has been attributed and 29 per cent of them from rural areas to urban migration.

17. a By 2050, an estimated two-thirds of the world's population will live in urban areas, imposing even more pressure on the space infrastructure and resources of cities, which are manifested in terms of sanitary, health, crime problems and urban poverty.

18. d Air pollution causes various diseases related to respiratory, nervous and circulatory systems.

19. d • development of 'Ganga Grams' in Uttarakhand, UP, Bihar, Jharkhand and West Bengal,

20. d There are some other types of wastelands such as degraded shifting cultivation area, degraded land under plantation crops, degraded forests, degraded pastures, and mining and industrial wastelands.

PART – II

CHAPTER 1

Human Geography Nature and Scope

Chapter at Glance

- "Human geography is the synthetic study of relationship between human societies and earth's surface". - Ratzel.

- "Human geography is the study of "the changing relationship between the unresting man and the unstable earth." - Ellen C. Semple

Nature Of Human Geography

- Human geography studies the inter-relationship between the physical environment and sociocultural environment created by human beings through mutual interaction with each other.

- These elements are landforms, soils, climate, water, natural vegetation and diverse flora and fauna.

- Houses, villages, cities, road-rail networks, industries, farms, ports, items of our daily use and all other elements of material culture have been created by human beings using the resources provided by the physical environment.

- While physical environment has been greatly modified by human beings, it has also, in turn, impacted human lives.

Naturalization of Humans and Humanization of Nature

- Human beings interact with their physical environment with the help of technology.

- The knowledge about Nature is extremely important to develop technology and technology loosens the shackles of environment on human beings.

- In the early stages of their interaction with their natural environment humans were greatly influenced by it.

- They adapted to the dictates of Nature. This is so because the level of technology was very low and the stage of human social development was also primitive.

- This type of interaction between primitive human society and strong forces of nature was termed as environmental determinism.

- The people begin to understand their environment and the forces of nature with the passage of time.

- With social and cultural development, humans develop better and more efficient technology.

- They move from a state of necessity to a state of freedom. They create possibilities with the resources obtained from the environment.

- The imprints of human activities are created everywhere; health resorts on highlands, huge urban sprawls, fields, orchards and pastures in plains and rolling hills, ports on the coasts, oceanic routes on the oceanic surface and satellites in the space. The earlier scholars termed this as possibilism.

- A geographer, Griffith Taylor introduced another concept which reflects a middle path (MadhyamMarg) between the two ideas of environmental determinism and possibilism. He termed it as Neodeterminism or stop and go determinism.

- Possibilities can be created within the limits which do not damage the environment and there is no free run without accidents.

- The free run which the developed economies attempted to take has already resulted in the greenhouse effect, ozone layer depletion, global warming, receding glaciers and degrading lands.

- The neo-determinism conceptually attempts to bring a balance nullifying the 'either' 'or' dichotomy.

Human Geography through the Corridors of Time

- The process of adaptation, adjustment with and modification of the environment started with the appearance of human beings over the surface of the earth in different ecological niches.

- ❖ Earlier there was little interaction between different societies and the knowledge about each other was limited.
- ❖ Travellers and explorers used to disseminate information about the areas of their visits. Navigational skills were not developed and voyages were fraught with dangers.
- ❖ The late fifteenth century witnessed attempts of explorations in Europe and slowly the myths and mysteries about countries and people started to open up.

Fields and Sub-fields of Human Geography

- ❖ Human geography assumes a highly inter-disciplinary nature.
- ❖ It develop close interface with other sister disciplines in social sciences in order to understand and explain human elements on the surface of the earth.
- ❖ With the expansion of knowledge, new subfields emerge and it has also happened to human geography.

Human Geography and Sister Discipline of Social Sciences

Fields of Human Geography	Sub-fields	Interface with Sister Disciplines of Social Sciences
Social Geography	–	Social Sciences - Sociology
	Behavioural Geography	Psychology
	Geography of Social Well-being	Welfare Economics
	Geography of Leisure	Sociology
	Cultural Geography	Anthropology
	Gender Geography	Sociology, Anthropology, Women's Studies
	Historical Geography	History
	Medical Geography	Epidemology
Urban Geography	–	Urban Studies and Planning
Political Geography	–	Political Science
	Electoral Geography	Psephology
	Military Geography	Military Science
Population Geography	–	Demography
Settlement Geography	–	Urban /Rural Planning
Economic Geography	–	Economics
	Geography of Resources	Resource Economics
	Geography of Agriculture	Agricultural Sciences
	Geography of Industries	Industrial Economics
	Geography of Marketing	Business Studies, Economics, Commerce
	Geography of Tourism	Tourism and Travel Management
	Geography of International Trade	International Trade

Exercise

1. Which of the following are components of earth?
   I.   Nature
   II. Life forms
   III. Non living forms
   (a) I and II
   (b) II and III
   (c) I and III
   (d) All of the above

2. Choose the incorrect statement regarding geography:
   (a) It is an integrative discipline
   (b) It is study of the inter-relationship between humans and environment
   (c) It is subjected to dualism
   (d) It is not relevant in the present time due to the development of technology

3. Choose the incorrect match from the following pairs of phenomenon:
   (a) Face : Earth
   (b) Mouth : River
   (c) Neck : Glacier
   (d) Profile : Soil

4. "Human geography is the synthetic study of relationship between human societies and earth's surface". This definition of human geography was given by the following gepgrapher?
   (a) Ellen C. Semple
   (b) Ratzel
   (c) Paul Vidal de la Blache
   (d) Unanimous

5. Who described human geography as a changing relationship between unresting human being and unstable earth?
   (a) Emanuel Kant
   (b) Harry Hess
   (c) Paul Vidal de la Blache
   (d) Ellen C. Semple

6. What is important for interaction between human beings and physical environment?
   (a) Tools and weapons
   (b) Technology
   (c) Excavation
   (d) Geographers

7. The following developments were possible due to discovery of –
   I.   Understanding of concepts of friction and heat helped to discover fire
   II. Understanding of the secrets of DNA and genetics enabled to conquer many diseases
   III. The laws of aerodynamics to develop faster planes
   (a) Technology
   (b) Understanding of geography
   (c) Understanding of geographical phenomenon
   (d) All of the above

8. The interaction between primitive human society and strong forces of nature is known as –
   (a) Environmental upgradation
   (b) Environmental determinism
   (c) Ecological evolution
   (d) Human geography

9. Which of the following defines possibilism?
   I.   Health resorts on highlands
   II. Satellites in space
   III. Pastures in planes
   (a) I and III
   (b) II and III
   (c) I and II
   (d) All of the above

10. The concept of neodeterminism was introduced by –
    (a) Emanuel Kant
    (b) Ratzel
    (c) Griffith Taylor
    (d) None of the above

11. Which one of the following is not a source of geographical information?
    (a) Traveller's accounts
    (b) Old maps
    (c) Samples of rock materials from the moon
    (d) Ancient epics

12. Which one of the following is not an approach in human geography?
    (a) Areal differentiation
    (b) Quantitative revolution
    (c) Spatial organisation
    (d) Exploration and description

13. Which of the following statements are incorrect about neodeterminism?
    I.   There is no situation of absolute necessity
    II. No condition of absolute freedom presents
    (a) I only
    (b) II only
    (c) Both I and II
    (d) Neither I nor II

14. The free run of developed economies lead to the following –

    I.   Ozone layer depletion

    II. Global warming

    III. Degrading lands

    (a) III only   (b) I and II

    (c) II and III   (d) All of the above

15. Which of the following are dealt in humanistic school of thought in human geography?

    I.   Health

    II. House

    III. Poverty

    (a) I and II   (b) II and III

    (c) I and III   (d) All of the above

16. Which of the following approach of human geography describes the feature of encyclopaedic description of the area that formed an important aspect of the geographer's account?

    (a) Regional analysis

    (b) Areal differentiation

    (c) Exploration and description

    (d) Spatial organization

17. Assertion: With social and cultural development, humans develop better and more efficient technology.

    Reason: They create possibilities with the resources obtained from the environment.

    (a) Both A and R are true and R is the correct explanation of A

    (b) Both A and R are true and R is not the correct explanation of A

    (c) A is true and R is false

    (d) A is false and R is true

Read the following passage and answer the following questions 18 to 20:

Benda lives in the wilds of the AbujhMaad area of central India. His village consists of three huts deep in the wilds. Not even birds or stray dogs that usually crowd villages can be seen in these areas. Wearing a small loin cloth and armed with his axe he slowly surveys the penda (forest) where his tribe practices a primitive form of agriculture called shifting cultivation. Benda and his friends burn small patches of forest to clear them for cultivation. The ash is used for making the soil fertile. Benda is happy that the Mahua trees around him are in bloom. How lucky I am to be a part of this beautiful universe, he thinks as he looks up to see the Mahua, Palash and Sal trees that have sheltered him since childhood.

18. The passage suggests the idea of –

    (a) Humanisation of nature

    (b) Primitive society

    (c) Naturalization of nature

    (d) Primitive agricultural practice

19. Slash and burn method of cultivation is good for agriculture as it is –

    (a) Practiced by tribal community

    (b) Free from fertilizers

    (c) Less water retentive

    (d) Promoting primitive culture

20. Mahua, Palash and Sal trees are vegetation of –

    (a) Tropical evergreen forest

    (b) Alpine forest

    (c) Tropical moist deciduous type

    (d) All of the above

Answers

1. (a)   **2.** (d)   **3.** (c)   **4.** (b)   **5.** (d)   **6.** (b)   **7.** (a)   **8.** (b)   **9.** (d)   **10.** (c)

11. (c)   **12.** (b)   **13.** (c)   **14.** (d)   **15.** (a)   **16.** (c)   **17.** (b)   **18.** (c)   **19.** (b)   **20.** (c)

CHAPTER 2

The World Population

Distribution, Density and Growth

Pattern of population distribution

- The world at the beginning of 21stcentury recorded the presence of over 6 billion population.

- The world has many places where people are few and few place where people are very many

- Patterns of population distribution and density help us to understand the demographic characteristics of any area.

- The term population distribution refers to the way people are spaced over the earth's surface.

- Broadly, 90 per cent of the world population lives in about 10 per cent of its land area.

- The 10 most populous countries of the world contribute about 60 per cent of the world's population. Of these 10 countries, 6 are located in Asia.

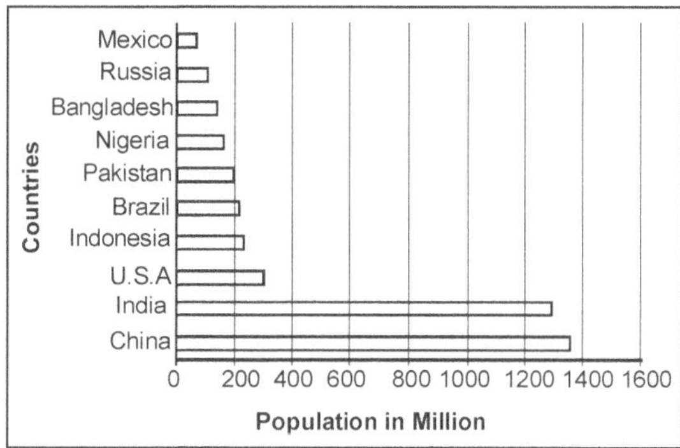

Fig. 2.1: Most Populous Countries

Density of Population

Density of Population = Population /Area

- This ratio is the density of population.

- It is usually measured in persons per sq km

- Asia has the highest density of population.

Factors Influencing the distribution of Population

Geographical Factors

- *Availability of water-* People prefer to live in areas where fresh water is easily

- *Landforms:* People prefer living on flat plains and gentle slopes.

- *Climate:*Areas with a comfortable climate, where there is not much seasonal variation attract more people.

- *Soils:* Fertile soils are important for agricultural and allied activities.

Economic Factors

- *Minerals:* Areas with mineral deposits attract industries.

- *Urbanisation:* Cities offer better employment opportunities, educational and medical facilities, better means of transport and communication.

- *Industrialisation:* Industrial belts provide job opportunities and attract large numbers of people.

Social and Cultural Factors

- Some places attract more people because they have religious or cultural significance.

Population Growth

- It is the change in number of inhabitants of a territory during a specific period of time.

- This change may be positive as well as negative.

- It can be expressed either in terms of absolute numbers or in terms of percentage.

- Population change in an area is an important indicator of economic development, social upliftment and historical and cultural background of the region.

Components of Population Change

- There are three components of population change – births, deaths and migration.

Births

- The crude birth rate (CBR) is expressed as number of live births in a year per thousand of population.

It is calculated as: $CBR = \dfrac{Bi}{P} \times 1000$

- CBR = Crude Birth Rate Bi = live births during the year; P = Mid year population of the area.

Deaths

- Crude Death Rate (CDR) is a simple method of measuring mortality of any area.
- CDR is expressed in terms of number of deaths in a particular year per thousand of population in a particular region

  CDR is calculated as: $CDR = \dfrac{D}{P} \times 1000$

- CDR = Crude Death Rate; D = Number of deaths; P = Estimated mid-year population of that year.
- Mortality rates are affected by the region's demographic structure, social advancement and levels of its economic development.

Migration

- It is another way by which the population size changes.
- When people move from one place to another, the place they move from is called the **Place of Origin** and the place they move to is called the **Place of Destination**.
- The place of origin shows a decrease in population while the population increases in the place of destination.

Doubling time of World Population

- Migration may be interpreted as a spontaneous effort to achieve a better balance between population and resources.
- Migration may be permanent, temporary or seasonal.
- It may take place from rural to rural areas, rural to urban areas, urban to urban areas and urban to rural areas.

Immigrant v/s Emigrant

- *Immigration:* Migrants who move into a new place are called Immigrants.
- *Emigration:* Migrants who move out of a place are called Emigrants.

Why people migrate

- People migrate for a better economic and social life.
- Factors that influence migration

There are two sets of factors that influence migration.

- The **Push** factors make the place of origin seem less attractive
- The **Pull** factors make the place of destination seem more attractive than the place of origin

Trends in Population growth

- The population on the earth is more than seven billion.
- In last few hundred years, population has increased at an alarming rate.

Table 2.2: Doubling Time of World Population

Period	Population	Time in which Population Doubles
10,000 B.C	5 million	
1650 A.D.	500 million	1,500 years
1804 A.D	1,000 million	154 years
1927 A.D.	2,000 million	123 years
1974 A.D.	4,000 million	47 years
2025 A.D.	8,000 million projected figure	51 years

Source: Demographic Year Book, 2009-10

- There is a great variation among regions in doubling their population.
- Developed countries take more time to double their population as compared to developing
- Most of the population growth is taking place in the developing world, where population is exploding.

Spatial Pattern of Population Change

- The growth of population is low in developed countries as compared to developing countries. There is negative correlation between economic development and population growth.

The concept of annual rate of population

- When a small annual rate is applied to a very large population, it will lead to a large population change.
- Even if the growth rate continues to decline, the total population grows each year.
- The infant mortality rate may have increased as has the death rate during childbirth.

Impact of Population Change

- Population growth beyond a certain level leads to problems.
- Population decline is also a matter of concern.

Demographic Transition

- Demographic transition theory can be used to describe and predict the future population of any area.
- Population of any region changes from high births and high deaths to low births and low deaths as society progresses from rural agrarian and illiterate to urban industrial and literate society.
- These changes occur in stages which are collectively known as the **demographic cycle**

Population Control Measures

- Family planning is the spacing or preventing the birth of children.
- Access to family planning services is a significant factor in limiting population growth and improving women's health.
- Propaganda, free availability of contraceptives and tax disincentives for large families are some of the measures which can help population control.

Exercise

1. Fill in the blanks

   90 ___________-per cent of the world population lives in about___________ 10 per cent of its land area.

   (a) 80, 20   (b) 85, 15

   (c) 90, 10   (d) None of the above

2. Consider the following statements

   1. The 10 most populous countries of the world contribute about 60 per cent of the world's population.

   2. Out of 10 most populous countries, 6 are located in Asia.

   Choose the correct answer from the codes given below

   (a) 1 only   (b) 2 only

   (c) Both 1 and 2   (d) Neither 1 nor 2

3. The growth of population is low in _______________ countries as compared to _____________ countries

   (a) developing, developed

   (b) developed, developing

   (c) coastal, mainland

   (d) none of the above

4. Demographic transition theory can be used to describe and predict the

   (a) birth rate

   (b) future population of any area.

   (c) future population of a particular area

   (d) death rate

5. Migrants who move into a new place are called

   (a) Immigrants   (b) Emigrants

   (c) Nomads   (d) Heralds

6. Population of any region changes from high births and high deaths to low births and low deaths as society progresses from rural agrarian and illiterate to urban industrial and literate society. These changes occur in stages which are collectively known as the

   (a) Density of population

   (b) Demographic cycle Explanations

   (c) Population Growth

   (d) None of the above

7. What are the sets of factors that influence migration?

   (a) Push Factor   (b) Pull Factor

   (c) Both 1 and 2   (d) Neither 1 nor 2

8. Find the true statement

   (a) When a small annual rate is applied to a very large population, it will lead to a large population change.

   (b) If the growth rate continues to decline, the total population decline each year.

   (c) When a large annual rate is applied to a very large population, it will lead to a large population change.

   (d) If the growth rate continues to increase, the total population also grows each year.

9. There is _______________ correlation between economic development and population growth.

   (a) Negative   (b) Positive

   (c) Inversely   (d) None of the above

10. Migrants who move out of a place are called

    (a) Emigrants.

    (b) Immigrants

    (c) Nomads

    (d) Heralds

11. Find the incorrect statement

    (a) There is a great variation among regions in doubling their population.

    (b) Developed countries take more time to double their population as compared to developing

    (c) Most of the population growth is taking place in the developing world, where population is exploding.

    (d) None of the above

12. Consider the following formula of Crude Death Rate

    CDR is calculated as $CDR = \dfrac{D}{P} \times 1000$

    Here P represents

    (a) Estimated mid-year population of that year.

    (b) Estimated population of that year.

    (c) Population of a particular area

    (d) None of the above

13. Mortality rate of a region is affected by which of the following factors?

    (a) region's demographic structure

    (b) social advancement

    (c) levels of its economic development.

    (d) all of the above

14. What are the components of population change

    (a) births

    (b) deaths

    (c) migration

    (d) all of the above

15. Consider the following formular about Crude birth rate (CBR)

$$CBR = \frac{Bi}{P} \times 1000$$

Here Bi represents

    (a) Mid year population of the area.

    (b) live births during the year

    (c) Crude Birth Rate

    (d) Both (a) and (b)

Answers

1. (c)   **2.** (c)   **3.** (b)   **4.** (b)   **5.** (a)   **6.** (b)   **7.** (c)   **8.** (a)   **9.** (*)   **10.** (a)

11. (d)   **12.** (a)   **13.** (d)   **14.** (d)   **15.** (b)

Explanations

2. c The 10 most populous countries of the world contribute about 60 per cent of the world's population. Of these 10 countries, 6 are located in Asia.

5. a Immigration: Migrants who move into a new place are called Immigrants.

7. c • The **Push** factors make the place of origin seem less attractive

    • The **Pull** factors make the place of destination seem more attractive than the place of origin

10. a Emigration: Migrants who move out of a place are called Emigrants

12. a • CDR = Crude Death Rate; D = Number of deaths; P = Estimated mid-year population of that year.

14. d • There are three components of population change – births, deaths and migration.

15. b • The crude birth rate (CBR) is expressed as number of live births in a year per thousand of population.

    • CBR = Crude Birth Rate Bi = live births during the year; P = Mid year population of the area.

Your Notes :

Population Composition

Population Composition

- People of any country are diverse in many respects.
- People can be distinguished by their age, sex and their place of residence.
- Other distinguishing attributes of the population are occupation, education and life expectancy.

Sex Composition

- The ratio between the number of women and men in the population is called the Sex Ratio.

In some countries it is calculated by using the formula:

- Male Population/ Female Population × 1000

  or the number of males per thousand females.

In India, the sex ratio is worked out using the formula:

- Female Population/ Male Population × 1000

  or the number of females per thousand males.

- The sex ratio is an important information about the status of women in a country.
- In regions where gender discrimination is rampant, the sex ratio is bound to be unfavourable to women.
- Such areas are those where the practice of female foeticide, female infanticide and domestic violence against women areprevalent.
- Oneof thereasonscouldbelower socio-economic status of women in these areas.
- More women in the population does not mean they have a better status.
- It could be that the men might have migrated to other areas for employment.

Sex ratio

- On an average, the world population reflects a sex ratio of 102 males per 100 females.
- The highest sex ratio in the world has been recorded in Latvia where there are 85 males per 100 females.
- In contrast, in Qatar there are 311 males per 100 females.

- In general, Asia has a low sex ratio.
- Countries like China, India, Saudi Arabia, Pakistan, Afghanistan have a lower sex ratio.
- On the other extreme is greater part of Europe (including Russia) where males are in minority. A deficit of males in the populations of many European countries is attributed to better status of women, and an excessively male-dominated out-migration to different parts of the world in the past.

Age Structure

- Age structure represents the number of people of different age groups.
- This is an important indicator of population composition
- A large size of population in the age group of 15- 59 indicates a large working population.
- Population above 60 years represents an ageing population which requires more expenditure on health care facilities.
- High proportion of young population would mean that the region has a high birth rate and the population is youthful.

Age-Sex Pyramid

- The age-sex structure of a population refers to the number of females and males in different age groups.
- A population pyramid is used to show the age-sex structure of the population.
- The shape of the population pyramid reflects the characteristics of the population.

Expanding Populations

- The age-sex pyramid is a triangular shaped pyramid with a wide base and is typical of less developed countries.
- These have larger populations in lower age groups due to high birth rates.
- If you construct the pyramids for Bangladesh and Mexico, it would look the same

Constant Population

- Australia's age-sex pyramid is bell shaped and tapered towards the top.
- This shows birth and death rates are almost equal leading to a near constant population.

Declining Populations

- The Japan pyramid has a narrow base and a tapered top showing low birth and death rates.
- The population growth in developed countries is usually zero or negative.

Rural Urban Composition

- The division of population into rural and urban is based on the residence.
- Rural and urban life styles differ from each other in terms of their livelihood and social conditions.
- The age-sex-occupational structure, density of population and level of development vary between rural and urban areas.
- The criteria for differentiating rural and urban population varies from country to country.
- In general terms rural areas are those where people are engaged in primary activities and urban areas are those when majority of the working population is engaged in non-primary activities.
- In Western countries, males outnumber females in rural areas and females outnumber the males in urban areas.
- In countries like Nepal, Pakistan and India the case is reverse.
- The excess of females in urban areas of U.S.A., Canada and Europe is the result of influx of females from rural areas to avail of the vast job opportunities.
- The sex ratio in Asian urban areas remains male dominated due to the predominance of male migration.

- In India, female participation in farming activity in rural area is fairly high.
- Shortage of housing, high cost of living, paucity of job opportunities and lack of security in cities, discourage women to migrate from rural to urban areas.

Literacy

- Proportion of literate population of a country in an indicator of its socio-economic development
- In India – literacy rate denotes the percentage of population above 7 years of age, who is able to read, write and have the ability to do arithmetic calculations with understanding.

Occupational Structure

- The working population (i.e. women and men of the age group – 15 to 59) take part in various occupations ranging from agriculture, forestry, fishing, manufacturing construction, commercial transport, services, communication and other unclassified services.
- Agriculture, forestry, fishing and mining are classified as primary activities manufacturing as secondary, trade, transport, communication and other services as tertiary and the jobs related to research, information technology and developing ideas as quaternary activities.
- The proportion of working population engaged in these four sectors is a good indicator of the levels of economic development of a nation.
- This is because only a developed economy with industries and infrastructure can accommodate more workers in the secondary, tertiary and quaternary sector.
- If the economy is still in the primitive stages, then the proportion of people engaged in primary activities world be high as it involves extraction of natural resources.

Exercise

1. Consider the following statements about Population ageing

   1. Population ageing is the process by which the share of the older population becomes proportionally larger.
   2. In most of the developed countries of the world, population in higher age groups has increased due to increased life expectancy.

   Choose the correct answer from the codes given below

   (a) 1 only

   (b) 2 only

   (c) Both 1 and 2

   (d) Neither 1 nor 2

2. In India – literacy rate denotes the percentage of population above________ of age, who is able to read, write and have the ability to do arithmetic calculations with understanding.

   (a) 8 years

   (b) 7 years

   (c) 5 years

   (d) 9 years

3. The Japan pyramid has a____________ showing low birth and death rates.

   (a) narrow base and a tapered top

   (b) tapered base and a narrow top

   (c) narrow base and inclined top

   (d) None of the above

4. The population growth in developed countries is usually

   (a) zero

   (b) negative

   (c) Positive

   (d) Both a and b

5. Australia's age-sex pyramid is bell shaped and tapered towards the top. This shows birth and death rates are almost equal leading to a near ________

   (a) Variable population

   (b) Constant population.

   (c) Expanding population

   (d) None of the above

6. Consider the following statement about sex ratio

   1. On an average, the world population reflects a sex ratio of 102 males per 100 females.
   2. The highest sex ratio in the world has been recorded in Latvia where there are 85 males per 100 females.

   Choose the correct answer from the codes given below

   (a) 1 only

   (b) 2 only

   (c) Both 1 and 2

   (d) Neither 1 nor 2

7. Which of the following countries have lower sex ratio?

   (a) China   (b) India

   (c) Pakistan   (d) All of the above

8. Which one of the following has caused the sex ratio of the United Arab Emirates to be low?

   (a) Selective migration of male working population

   (b) High birth rate of males

   (c) Low birth rate of females

   (d) High out migration of females

9. Which one of the following figures represents the working age group of the population?

   (a) 15 to 65 years

   (b) 15 to 66 years

   (c) 15 to 64 years

   (d) 15 to 59 years

10. Agriculture, forestry, fishing and mining are classified as

    (a) primary activities

    (b) secondary activities

    (c) tertiary activities

    (d) None of the above

11. Consider the following statements

    1. In Western countries, males outnumber females in rural areas and females outnumber the males in urban areas
    2. The excess of females in urban areas of U.S.A., Canada and Europe is the result of influx of females from rural areas

    Choose the correct answer from the codes given below

    (a) 1 only

    (b) 2 only

    (c) Both 1 and 2

    (d) Neither 1 nor 2

12. Consider the following formula

$$\frac{\text{Male Population}}{\text{Female Population}} \times 1000$$

This formula is used to calculate

(a) Demographic characteristic.

(b) Sex ration

(c) Sex composition

(d) None of the above

13. Which of the following continents has lowest sex ratio.

(a) Asia

(b) Africa

(c) North America

(d) South America

14. It represents the number of people of different age groups. This is an important indicator of population composition, since a large size of population in the age group of 15- 59 indicates a large working population.

A greater proportion of population above 60 years represents an ageing population which requires more expenditure on health care facilities.

Similarly high proportion of young population would mean that the region has a high birth rate and the population is youthful.

The above information best describes which o the following terminologies?

(a) Age structure   (b) Sex – pyramid

(c) Expanding nature   (d) Constant population

Answers

1. (c)   **2.** (b)   **3.** (a)   **4.** (d)   **5.** (b)   **6.** (c)   **7.** (d)   **8.** (*)   **9.** (d)   **10.** (a)

11. (d)   **12.** (b)   **13.** (a)   **14.** (a)

Explanations

7.   d   In general, Asia has a low sex ratio. Countries like China, India, Saudi Arabia, Pakistan, Afghanistan have a lower sex ratio.

Human Development

Growth and Development

Both growth and development refer to changes over a period of time.

Growth

- It is quantitative and value neutral.
- It may have a positive or a negative sign.
- This means that the change may be either positive (showing an increase) or negative (indicating a decrease).

Development

- It means a qualitative change which is always value positive.
- This means that development cannot take place unless there is an increment or addition to the existing conditions.
- Development occurs when positive growth takes place.
- Yet, positive growth does not always lead to development.
- Development occurs when there is a positive change in quality.
- eg. For example, if the population of a city grows but basic facilities remain the same, then this growth has not been accompanied by development.

Human Development

- The concept of human development was introduced by Dr Mahbub-ul-Haq.
- Dr Haq has described human development as development that enlarges people's choices and improves their lives.
- People are central to all development under this concept.
- These choices are not fixed but keep on changing.
- The basic goal of development is to create conditions where people can live meaningful lives.
- This means that people must be healthy, be able to develop their talents, participate in society and be free to achieve their goals.
- Leading a long and healthy life, being able to gain knowledge and having enough means to be able to live a decent life are the most important aspects of human development.
- Therefore, access to resources, health and education are the key areas in human development.
- Building people's capabilities in the areas of health, education and access to resources is therefore, important in enlarging their choices.

The Four Pillara of Human Development

- The idea of human development is supported by the concepts of **equity, sustainability, productivity** and **empowerment**.
- Equity refers to making equal access to opportunities available to everybody.
- Sustainability means continuity in the availability of opportunities.
- Productivity here means human labour productivity or productivity in terms of human work.
- Empowerment means to have the power to make choices. Such power comes from increasing freedom and capability.

Approaches to Human Development

- There are many ways of looking at the problem of human development.

Some of the important approaches are:

a) The income approach;

b) The welfare approach;

c) Minimum needs approach; and

d) Capabilities approach

Measuring Human Development

- The human development index (HDI) ranks the countries based on their performance in the key areas of health, education and access to resources.
- These rankings are based on a score between 0 to 1 that a country earns from its record in the key areas of human development.
- The indicator chosen to assess health is the life expectancy at birth.
- A higher life expectancy means that people have a greater chance of living longer and healthier lives.

- The adult literacy rate and the gross enrolment ratio represent access to knowledge.
- The number of adults who are able to read and write and the number of children enrolled in schools show how easy or difficult it is to access knowledge in a particular country.
- Access to resources is measured in terms of purchasing power (in U.S. dollars).
- Each of these dimensions is given a weightage of 1/3.
- The human development index is a sum total of the weights assigned to all these dimensions.
- The closer a score is to one, the greater is the level of human development.
- Therefore, a score of 0.983 would be considered very high while 0.268 would mean a very low level of human development.
- The human development index measures **attainments** in human development.
- It reflects what has been achieved in the key areas of human development.
- Yet it is not the most reliable measure.
- This is because it does not say anything about the distribution.

Human poverty index

- The human poverty index is related to the human development index. This index measures the **shortfall** in human development

- It is a non-income measure.
- The probability of not surviving till the age of 40, the adult illiteracy rate, the number of people who do not have access to clean water, and the number of small children who are underweight are all taken into account to show the shortfall in human development in any region.
- Often the human poverty index is more revealing than the human development index.

International Comparisions

- Size of the territory and per capita income are not directly related to human development.
- Smaller countries have done better than larger ones in human development.
- Similarly, relatively poorer nations have been ranked higher than richer neighbours in terms of human development.
- For example, Sri Lanka, Trinidad and Tobago have a higher rank than India in the human development index despite having smaller economies.
- Similarly, within India, Kerala performs much better than Punjab and Gujarat in human development despite having lower per capita income.
- Countries can be classified into four groups on the basis of the human development scores earned by them (HDR 2020)

Level of Human Development	Score in Development Index	Number of Countries
Very High	above 0.800	66
High	between 0.700 up to 0.799	53
Medium	between 0.550 up to 0.699	37
Low	below 0.549	33

Human Development – other aspects

- Countries with higher human development are those where a lot of investment in the social sector has taken place.
- Many of the countries with a high human development score are located in Europe and represent the industrialised western world.
- To understand why a particular region keeps reporting low or high levels of human development it is important to look at the pattern of government expenditure on the social sector.
- The political environment of the country and the amount of freedom people have is also important.
- Countries with high levels of human development invest more in the social sectors and are generally free from political turmoil and instability.
- Distribution of the country's resources is also far more equitable.
- On the other hand, places with low levels of human development tend to spend more on defence rather than social sectors.
- This shows that these countries tend to be located in areas of political instability and have not been able to initiate accelerated economic development

Exercise

1. Find the incorrect statement about growth

  (a) Growth is quantitative and value neutral

  (b) Growth always have a positive sign

  (c) It refer to changes over a period of time

  (d) Both (a) and (b)

2. Which of the following approaches to Human Development is the oldest one

  (a) The income approach (b) The welfare approach

  (c) Basic needs approach (d) Capabilities approach

3. Which of the following is the only country in the world to officially proclaim the Gross National Happiness (GNH) as the measure of the country's progress.

  (a) Bhutan   (b) Nepal

  (c) Sri Lanka   (d) None of the above

4. The Human Development index has been published by which of the following organisations?

  (a) United Nations Development Programme (UNDP)

  (b) UNESCO

  (c) UNEP

  (d) World Bank

5. Which of the following are the two important indices to measure human development used by the UNDP.

  (a) Human Development index

  (b) Human Poverty index

  (c) Both (a) and (b)

  (d) Neither(a) nor (b)

6. Consider the following statements about Development

  1. It means a qualitative change which is always value positive

  2. It cannot take place unless there is an increment or addition to the existing conditions

  3. Positive growth does not always lead to development.

  Choose the correct answer from the codes given below

  (a) 1 and 2   (b) 1, 2 and 3

  (c) 1 and 3   (d) 2 and 3

7. Pakistani economist Dr Mahbub-ul-Haq created the Human Development Index in ________-

  (a) 1991   (b) 1990

  (c) 1989   (d) 2004

8. The above statement has been given by which of the following economists?

  (a) Dr Mahbub-ul-Haq   (b) Prof Amartya Sen

  (c) Prof S.N jha   (d) Both (a) and (b)

9. Which of the following approaches to Human Development was initiallyproposed by the International Labour Organisation (ILO).

  (a) The income approach

  (b) The welfare approach

  (c) Basic needs approach

  (d) Capabilities approach

10. Consider the following statements about the human development index (HDI)

  1. HDI ranks the countries based on their performance in the key areas of health, education and access to resources

  2. These rankings are based on a score between 0 to 100

  Choose the correct answer from the codes given below

  (a) 1 only   (b) 2 only

  (c) Both 1 and 2   (d) Neither 1 nor 2

11. What are the four pillars of Human Development

  1. equity   2. sustainability

  3. productivity   4. empowerment.

  5. economic activity   6. Health

  Choose the correct answer from the codes given below

  (a) 1, 2, 5 and 6   (b) 1, 2, 3 and 4

  (c) 2, 3, 4 and 5   (d) 1, 2, 4 and 5

12. To have _____________ human development, each generation must have the same opportunities. All environmental, financial and human resources must be used keeping in mind the future. Misuse of any of these resources will lead to fewer opportunities for future generations.

  (a) Sustainable   (b) Productive

  (c) equity   (d) None of the above

13. Consider the following statements about Empowerment

  1. Empowerment means to have the power to make choices

  2. Good governance and people-oriented policies are required to empower people.

Choose the correct answer from the codes given below

(a) 1 only

(b) 2 only

(c) Both 1 and 2

(d) Neither 1 nor 2

14. If the population of a city grows from one lakh to two lakhs over a period of time, we say the city has grown. However, if a facilities like housing, provision of basic services and other characteristics remain the same, then this __________ has not been accompanied by ___________-

(a) Growth , Development

(b) Development, growth

(c) Growth, empowerment

(d) equality, empowerment

15. Which of the following are the important approachesof human development

1. The income approach

2. The welfare approach

3. Minimum needs approach

4. Capabilities approach

Choose the correct answer from the codes given below

(a) 1 and 2

(b) 1, 2 and 3

(c) 1 and 4

(d) 1, 2, 3 and 4

16. Which of the following approaches to Human Developmentis associated with Prof. Amartya Sen.

(a) The income approach

(b) The welfare approach

(c) Minimum needs approach

(d) Capabilities approach

17. He saw an increase in freedom (or decrease in unfreedom) as the main objective of development. Interestingly, increasing freedoms is also one of the most effective ways of bringing about development. His work explores the role of social and political institutions and processes in increasing freedom

The above statement represents the work of which of the following economists?

(a) Dr Mahbub-ul-Haq

(b) Prof Amartya Sen

(c) Abhijit Banerjee

(d) None of the above

18. Access to which of the following parameters are the key areas in human development.

1. resources

2. health

3. education

4. Home

Choose the correct answer from the codes given below

(a) 1 and 2

(b) 1, 2 and 4

(c) 1, 2 and 3

(d) 1, 2, 3 and 4

19. Which one of the following best describes development?

(a) an increase in size

(b) a positive change in quality

(c) a constant in size

(d) a simple change in the quality

20. Countries can be classified into which of the following groups on the basis of the human development scores earned by them?

1. Very High

2. High

3. Medium

4. Low

Choose the correct answer from the codes given below

(a) 1 and 2

(b) 1, 2 and 4

(c) 1, 2 and 3

(d) 1, 2, 3 and 4

Answers

1. (b)   **2.** (a)   **3.** (a)   **4.** (a)   **5.** (c)   **6.** (b)   **7.** (b)   **8.** (a)   **9.** (c)   **10.** (a)

11. (b)   **12.** (a)   **13.** (c)   **14.** (a)   **15.** (d)   **16.** (d)   **17.** (b)   **18.** (c)   **19.** (b)   **20.** (d)

Explanations

1. b • It may have a positive or a negative sign. This means that the change may be either positive (showing an increase) or negative (indicating a decrease).

3. a • Bhutan is the only country in the world to officially proclaim the Gross National Happiness (GNH) as the measure of the country's progress.

4. a • Since 1990, the United Nations Development Programme (UNDP) has been publishing the Human Development Report every year.

5. c • The Human Development index and the Human Poverty index are two important indices to measure human development used by the UNDP.

6. b • Development occurs when positive growth takes place. Yet, positive growth does not always lead to development. Development occurs when there is a positive change in quality.

7. b • Human development enlarges people's choices and improves their lives. People are central to all development under this concept. These choices are not fixed but keep on changing. The basic goal of development is to create conditions where people can live meaningful lives. A meaningful life is not just a long one. It must be a life with some purpose. This means that people must be healthy, be able to develop their talents, participate in society and be free to achieve their goals.

10. a • The human development index (HDI) ranks the countries based on their performance in the key areas of health, education and access to resources. These rankings are based on a score between 0 to 1 that a country earns from its record in the key areas of human development.

• The indicator chosen to assess health is the life expectancy at birth. A higher life expectancy means that people have a greater chance of living longer and healthier lives.

11. b • Just as any building is supported by pillars, the idea of human development is supported by the concepts of **equity, sustainability, productivity** and **empowerment**

12. a • Sustainability means continuity in the availability of opportunities. To have sustainable human development, each generation must have the same opportunities. All environmental, financial and human resources must be used keeping in mind the future. Misuse of any of these resources will lead to fewer opportunities for future generations.

13. c • Empowerment means to have the power to make choices. Such power comes from increasing freedom and capability. Good governance and people-oriented policies are required to empower people. The empowerment of socially and economically disadvantaged groups is of special importance.

15. d • There are many ways of looking at the problem of human development. Some of the important approaches are: (a) The income approach; (b) The welfare approach; (c) Minimum needs approach; and (d) Capabilities approach

16. d • This approach is associated with Prof. Amartya Sen. Building human capabilities in the areas of health, education and access to resources is the key to increasing human development.

18. c • access to resources, health and education are the key areas in human development.

Your Notes :

Primary Activities

Primary Activities

- Human activities which generate income are known as *economic activities.*
- Economic activities are broadly grouped into primary, secondary, tertiary and quaternary activities.
- Primary activities are directly dependent on environment as these refer to utilisation of earth's resources such as land, water, vegetation, building materials and minerals.
- It, thus includes, hunting and gathering, pastoral activities, fishing, forestry, agriculture, and mining and quarrying.

Hunting and Gathering

The earliest human beings subsisted on:

a) animals which they hunted; and

b) the edible plants which they gathered from forests in the vicinity.

- Primitive societies depended on wild animals.
- People located in very cold and extremely hot climates survived on hunting.
- Gathering and hunting are the oldest economic activity known.
- Gathering is practised in regions with harsh climatic conditions.
- It often involves primitive societies, who extract, both plants and animals to satisfy their needs for food, shelter and clothing.
- This type of activity requires a small amount of capital investment and operates at very low level of technology.
- The yield per person is very low and little or no surplus is produced.

Gathering is practised in:

i. high latitude zones which include northern Canada, northern Eurasia and southern Chile;

ii. Low latitude zones such as the Amazon Basin, tropical Africa, Northern fringe of Australia and the interior parts of Southeast Asia

- In modern times some gathering is market- oriented and has become commercial.
- Gatherers collect valuable plants such as leaves, barks of trees and medicinal plants and after simple processing sell the products in the market.
- Gathering has little chance of becoming important at the global level.

Pastoralism

- People living in different climatic conditions selected and domesticated animals found in those regions.
- Depending on the geographical factors, and technological development, animal rearing today is practised either at the subsistence or at the commercial level.

Nomadic Herding

- Nomadic herding or pastoral nomadism is a primitive subsistence activity, in which the herders rely on animals for food, clothing, shelter, tools and transport.
- They move from one place to another along with their livestock, depending on the amount and quality of pastures and water.
- Each nomadic community occupies a well-identified territory as a matter of tradition.
- A wide variety of animals is kept in different regions.
- In tropical Africa, cattle are the most important livestock, while in Sahara and Asiatic deserts, sheep, goats and camel are reared.
- In the mountainous areas of Tibet and Andes, yak and llamas and in the Arctic and sub Arctic areas, reindeer are the most important animals.
- Pastoral nomadism is associated with three important regions.
- The core region extends from the Atlantic shores of North Africa eastwards across the Arabian peninsula into Mongolia and Central China.
- The second region extends over the tundra region of Eurasia.
- In the southern hemisphere there are small areas in South-west Africa and on the island of Madagascar

- The process of migration from plain areas to pastures on mountains during summers and again from mountain pastures to plain areas during winters is known as *transhumance.*

- In mountain regions, such as Himalayas, Gujjars, Bakarwals, Gaddis and Bhotiyas migrate from plains to the mountains in summers and to the plains from the high altitude pastures in winters.

- Similarly, in the tundra regions, the nomadic herders move from south to north in summers and from north to south in winters.

- The number of pastoral nomads has been decreasing and the areas operated by them shrinking.

- This is due to (a) imposition of political boundaries; (b) new settlement plans by different countries.

Commercial Livestock Rearing

- Unlike nomadic herding, commercial livestock rearing is more organised and capital intensive.

- Commercial livestock ranching is essentially associated with western cultures and is practised on permanent ranches.

- These ranches cover large areas and are divided into a number of parcels, which are fenced to regulate the grazing.

- This is a specialised activity in which only one type of animal is reared.

- Important animals include sheep, cattle, goats and horses.

- Products such as meat, wool, hides and skin are processed and packed scientifically and exported to different world markets.

- Rearing of animals in ranching is organised on a scientific basis.

- The main emphasis is on breeding, genetic improvement, disease control and health care of the animals.

- New Zealand, Australia, Argentina, Uruguay and United States of America are important countries where commercial livestock rearing is practised

Agriculture

The following are the main agricultural systems.

Subsistence Agriculture

- Subsistence agriculture is one in which the farming areas consume all, or nearly so, of the products locally grown. It can be grouped in two categories — Primitive Subsistence Agriculture and Intensive Subsistence Agriculture.

Primitive Subsistence Agriculture

- Primitive subsistence agriculture or shifting cultivation is widely practised by many tribes in the tropics, especially in Africa, south and central America and south east Asia

- The vegetation is usually cleared by fire, and the ashes add to the fertility of the soil. Shifting cultivation is thus, also called **slash and burn agriculture**.

- The cultivated patches are very small and cultivation is done with very primitive tools such as sticks and hoes.

- After sometime (3 to 5 years) the soil looses its fertility and the farmer shifts to another parts and clears other patch of the forest for cultivation.

- The farmer may return to the earlier patch after sometime. One of the major problems of shifting cultivation is that the cycle of *jhum* becomes less and less due to loss of fertility in different parcels.

- It is prevalent in tropical region in different names, e.g. **Jhuming** in North eastern states of India, **Milpa** in central America and Mexico and **Ladang** in Indonesia and Malaysia.

Intensive Subsistence Agriculture

- This type of agriculture is largely found in densely populated regions of monsoon Asia.

- Basically, there are two types of intensive subsistence agriculture.

  (i) *Intensive subsistence agriculture dominated by wet paddy cultivation:*

    - This type of agriculture is characterised by dominance of the rice crop.

    - Land holdings are very small due to the high density of population.

    - Farmers work with the help of family labour leading to intensive use of land.

    - Use of machinery is limited and most of the agricultural operations are done by manual labour.

    - Farm yard manure is used to maintain the fertility of the soil.

    - In this type of agriculture, the yield per unit area is high but per labour productivity is low.

  (ii) *Intensive subsidence agriculture dominated by crops other than paddy:*

    - Due to the difference in relief, climate, soil and some of the other geographical factors, it is not practical to grow paddy in many parts of monsoon Asia.

- Wheat, soyabean, barley and sorghum are grown in northern China, Manchuria, North Korea and North Japan.
- In India wheat is grown in western parts of the Indo-Gangetic plains and millets are grown in dry parts of western and southern India.
- Most of the characteristics of this type of agriculture are similar to those dominated by wet paddy except that irrigation is often used.

Plantation Agriculture

- It was introduced by the Europeans in colonies situated in the tropics.
- Some of the important plantation crops are tea, coffee, cocoa, rubber, cotton, oil palm, sugarcane, bananas and pineapples.
- The characteristic features of this type of farming are large estates or plantations, large capital investment, managerial and technical support, scientific methods of cultivation, single crop specialisation, cheap labour, and a good system of transportation which links the estates to the factories and markets for the export of the products.
- The French established cocoa and coffee plantations in west Africa.
- The British set up large tea gardens in India and Sri Lanka, rubber plantations in Malaysia and sugarcane and banana plantations in West Indies.
- Spanish and Americans invested heavily in coconut and sugarcane plantations in the Philippines.
- The Dutch once had monopoly over sugarcane plantation in Indonesia. Some coffee fazendas (large plantations) in Brazil are still managed by Europeans.

Extensive Commercial Grain Cultivation

- Commercial grain cultivation is practised in the interior parts of semi-arid lands of the mid- latitudes.
- Wheat is the principal crop, though other crops like corn, barley, oats and rye are also grown. The size of the farm is very large, therefore entire operations of cultivation from ploughing to harvesting are mechanised
- There is low yield per acre but high yield per person.
- This type of agriculture is best developed in Eurasian steppes, the Canadian and American Prairies, the Pampas of Argentina, the Velds of South Africa, the Australian Downs and the Canterbury Plains of New Zealand.

Mixed Farming

- This form of agriculture is found in the highly developed parts of the world, e.g. North-western Europe, Eastern North America, parts of Eurasia and the temperate latitudes of Southern continents (Fig. 5.14).
- Mixed farms are moderate in size and usually the crops associated with it are wheat, barley, oats, rye, maize, fodder and root crops.
- Fodder crops are an important component of mixed farming.
- Crop rotation and intercropping play an important role in maintaining soil fertility.
- Equal emphasis is laid on crop cultivation and animal husbandry.
- Animals like cattle, sheep, pigs and poultry provide the main income along with crops.

Dairy Farming

- Dairy is the most advanced and efficient type of rearing of milch animals.
- It is highly capital intensive. It is highly labour intensive as it involves rigorous care in feeding and milching.
- It is practised mainly near urban and industrial centres which provide neighbourhood market for fresh milk and dairy products.
- There are three main regions of commercial dairy farming.
- The largest is North Western Europe the second is Canada and the third belt includes South Eastern Australia, New Zealand and Tasmania

Mediterranean Agriculture

- Mediterranean agriculture is highly specialised commercial agriculture.
- It is practised in the countries on either side of the Mediterranean sea in Europe and in north Africa from Tunisia to Atlantic coast
- This region is an important supplier of citrus fruits.
- **Viticulture** or grape cultivation is a speciality of the Mediterranean region.

Market Gardening and Horticulture

- Market gardening and horticulture specialise in the cultivation of high value crops such as vegetables, fruits and flowers, solely for the urban markets.
- Farms are small and are located where there are good transportation links with the urban centre where high income group of consumers is located.
- It is both labour and capital intensive and lays emphasis on the use of irrigation, HYV seeds, fertilisers, insecticides, greenhouses and artificial heating in colder regions.

- The regions where farmers specialise in vegetables only, the farming is know as **truck farming**.
- The distance of truck farms from the market is governed by the distance that a truck can cover overnight, hence the name truck farming.

Co-operative Farming

- A group of farmers form a co-operative society by pooling in their resources voluntarily for more efficient and profitable farming. Individual farms remain intact and farming is a matter of cooperative initiative.
- Co-operative societies help farmers, to procure all important inputs of farming, sell the products at the most favourable terms and help in processing of quality products at cheaper rates.

Collective Farming

- The basic principle behind this types of farming is based on social ownership of the means of production and collective labour.
- Collective farming or the model of **Kolkhoz** was introduced in erstwhile Soviet Union to improve upon the inefficiency of the previous methods of agriculture and to boost agricultural production for self-sufficiency.
- The farmers used to pool in all their resources like land, livestock and labour. However, they were allowed to retain very small plots to grow crops in order to meet their daily requirements.

Mining

- The discovery of minerals in the history of human development, is reflected in many stages in terms of copper age, bronze age and iron age

- The use of minerals in ancient times was largely confined to the making of tools, utensils and weapons.
- The actual development of mining began with the industrial revolution and its importance is continuously increasing.

Factors Affecting Mining Activity

The profitability of mining operations thus, depends on two main factors:

1. (i) Physical factors include the size, grade and the mode of occurrence of the deposits.
2. (ii) Economic factors such as the demand for the mineral, technology available and used, capital to develop infrastructure and the labour and transport costs.

Methods of Mining

- Depending on the mode of occurrence and the nature of the ore, mining is of two types: surface and underground mining.
- The surface mining also known as *open-cast* mining is the easiest and the cheapest way of mining minerals that occur close to the surface.
- Overhead costs such as safety precautions and equipment is relatively low in this method. The output is both large and rapid.
- When the ore lies deep below the surface, **underground mining method** (shaft method) has to be used.
- This method is risky. Poisonous gases, fires, floods and caving in lead to fatal accidents.

Exercise

1. Which one of the following is not a plantation crop?
   - (a) Coffee
   - (b) Wheat
   - (c) Sugarcane
   - (d) Rubber

2. In which one of the following countries co-operative farming was the most successful experiment?
   - (a) Denmark
   - (b) Netherlands
   - (c) Budapest
   - (d) Sweden

3. Growing of flowers is called:
   - (a) Truck farming
   - (b) Factory farming
   - (c) Mixed farming
   - (d) Floriculture

4. Viticultureor grape cultivation is a speciality of which of the following regions?
   - (a) Indian Ocean Region
   - (b) European regions
   - (c) Australian plains
   - (d) Mediterranean region.

5. The regions where farmers specialise in vegetables only, the farming is know as
   - (a) Agricultural farming
   - (b) Truck farming.
   - (c) Factory Farming
   - (d) None of the above

6. Which one of the following types of cultivation was developed by European colonists?
   - (a) Kolkoz
   - (b) Mixed farming
   - (c) Viticulture
   - (d) Plantation

7. In which one of the following regions is extensive commercial grain cultivation not practised?
   - (a) American Canadian prairies
   - (b) Pampas of Argentina
   - (c) European Steppes
   - (d) Amazon Basin

8. Which of the following are the oldest economic activities?
   - (a) Gathering
   - (b) hunting
   - (c) Fishing
   - (d) Both (a) and (b)

9. Commercial livestock rearing is practised in which of the following countries?
   - 1. New Zealand
   - 2. Australia
   - 3. Argentina
   - 4. Uruguay

   Choose the correct answer from the codes given below
   - (a) 1 and 2
   - (b) 2, 3 and 4
   - (c) 1 and 4
   - (d) 1, 2, 3 and 4

10. In which of the following types of agriculture is the farming of citrus fruit very important?
    - (a) Market gardening
    - (b) Mediterranean agriculture
    - (c) Plantation agriculture
    - (d) Co-operative farming

11. Which one type of agriculture amongst the following is also called 'slash and burn agriculture'?
    - (a) Extensive subsistence agriculture
    - (b) Primitive subsistence agriculture
    - (c) Extensive commercial grain cultivation
    - (d) Mixed farming

12. Consider the following statements about Nomadic Herding
    1. In this the herders rely on animals for food, clothing, shelter, tools and transport.
    2. They move from one place to another along with their livestock

    Choose the correct answer from the codes given below
    - (a) 1 only
    - (b) 2 only
    - (c) Both 1 and 2
    - (d) Neither 1 nor 2

13. The process of migration from plain areas to pastures on mountains during summers and again from mountain pastures to plain areas during winters is known as
    - (a) Transhumance
    - (b) Pastoralism
    - (c) Subsistence Gathering
    - (d) None of the above

14. Find the correct statement
    - (a) The French established cocoa and coffee plantations in west Africa.
    - (b) The British set up large tea gardens in India and Sri Lanka
    - (c) Spanish and Americans invested heavily in coconut and sugarcane plantations in the Philippines.
    - (d) All of the above

15. Consider the following statements about Extensive Commercial Grain Cultivation

1. It is practised in the interior parts of semi-arid lands of the mid-latitudes.
2. Wheat is the principal crop
3. The size of the farm is very large
4. There is low yield per acre but high yield per person.

Choose the correct answer from the codes given below

(a) 1 and 2
(b) 2, 3 and 4
(c) 1 and 4
(d) 1, 2, 3 and 4

16. Find the correct pair

Country	Grassland
(a) Argentina	Pampas
(b) South Africa	Velds
(c) Australia	Steppes
(d) New Zealand	Canterbury Plains

17. Human activities which generate income are known as *economic activities.*

Economic activities are broadly grouped into which of the following activities?

1. primary
2. secondary
3. tertiary
4. quaternary

Choose the correct answer from the codes given below

(a) 1 and 2
(b) 2, 3 and 4
(c) 1 and 4
(d) 1, 2, 3 and 4

18. Consider the following statement

This form of agriculture is found in the highly developed parts of the world, e.g. North-western Europe, Eastern North America, parts of Eurasia and the temperate latitudes of Southern continents

These farms are moderate in size and usually the crops associated with it are wheat, barley, oats, rye, maize, fodder and root crops.

The above statement best describes which type of farming?

(a) Truck farming
(b) Mixed Farming
(c) Grain Farming
(d) Dairy Farming

19. Market gardening and horticulture specialise in the cultivation of high value crops such as vegetables, fruits and flowers, solely for the _______________.

(a) Urban markets.
(b) Rural Markets
(c) Domestic Market
(d) International Market

20. Consider the following statements about a type of farming

- It is highly capital intensive.
- It is highly labour intensive as it involves rigorous care in feeding and milching.
- There is no off season during the year as in the case of crop raising.
- It is practised mainly near urban and industrial centres which provide neighbourhood market

The above information best describes which of the following types of farming?

(a) Truck farming
(b) Mixed Farming
(c) Grain Farming
(d) Dairy Farming

Answers

1. (b) **2.** (c) **3.** (d) **4.** (d) **5.** (b) **6.** (d) **7.** (d) **8.** (d) **9.** (d) **10.** (b)

11. (b) **12.** (c) **13.** (a) **14.** (d) **15.** (d) **16.** (c) **17.** (d) **18.** (b) **19.** (a) **20.** (d)

Explanations

8. d • Gathering and hunting are the oldest economic activity known. These are carried out at different levels with different orientations.

9. d • New Zealand, Australia, Argentina, Uruguay and United States of America are important countries where commercial livestock rearing is practised

11. b • Primitive subsistence agriculture or shifting cultivation is widely practised by many tribes in the tropics, especially in Africa, south and central America and south east Asia

12. c • Nomadic herding or pastoral nomadism is a primitive subsistence activity, in which the herders rely on animals for food, clothing, shelter, tools and transport. They move from one place to another along with their livestock, depending on the amount and quality of pastures and water. Each nomadic community occupies a well-identified territory as a matter of tradition

13. a • The process of migration from plain areas to pastures on mountains during summers and again from mountain pastures to plain areas during winters is known as *transhumance.*

14. d • The French established cocoa and coffee plantations in west Africa. The British set up large tea gardens in India and Sri Lanka, rubber plantations in Malaysia and sugarcane and banana plantations in West Indies.

15. d • Commercial grain cultivation is practised in the interior parts of semi-arid lands of the mid- latitudes.

• Wheat is the principal crop, though other crops like corn, barley, oats and rye are also grown.

• The size of the farm is very large, therefore entire operations of cultivation from ploughing to harvesting are mechanised

• There is low yield per acre but high yield per person.

16. c • Commercial grain cultivation is best developed in Eurasian steppes, the Canadian and American Prairies, the Pampas of Argentina, the Velds of South Africa, the Australian Downs and the Canterbury Plains of New Zealand. (Locate these areas on the world map).

17. d • Human activities which generate income are known as *economic activities.* Economic activities are broadly grouped into primary, secondary, tertiary and quaternary activities.

18. b • Fodder crops are an important component of mixed farming. Crop rotation and intercropping play an important role in maintaining soil fertility. Equal emphasis is laid on crop cultivation and animal husbandry. Animals like cattle, sheep, pigs and poultry provide the main income along with crops.

Your Notes :

Secondary Activities

* Secondary activities add value to natural resources by *transforming* raw materials into valuable products. Secondary activities, therefore, are concerned with manufacturing, processing and construction (infrastructure) industries.

* Manufacturing involves a full array of production from handicrafts to moulding iron and steel and stamping out plastic toys to assembling delicate computer components or space vehicles. In each of these processes, the common characteristics are the application of power, mass production of identical products and specialised labour in factory settings for the production of standardised commodities. Manufacturing may be done with modern power and machinery or it may still be very primitive. Most of the Third World countries still 'manufacture' in the literal sense of the term.

   * Characteristics of Modern Large Scale Manufacturing - Modern large scale manufacturing has the following characteristics:

   * *Specialisation of Skills/Methods of Production* - Under the 'craft' method factories produce only a few pieces which are made-to-order. So the costs are high. On the other hand, mass production involves production of large quantities of standardised parts by each worker performing only one task repeatedly.

   * *Mechanisation* - Mechanisation refers to using gadgets which accomplish tasks. Automation (without aid of human thinking during the manufacturing process) is the advanced stage of mechanisation. Automatic factories with feedback and closedloop computer control systems where machines are developed to 'think', have sprung up all over the world.

   * *Technological Innovation* - Technological innovations through research and development strategy are an important aspect of modern manufacturing for quality control, eliminating waste and inefficiency, and combating pollution.

   * *Organisational Structure and Stratification* - Modern manufacturing is characterised by:

      (i) a complex machine technology

      (ii) extreme specialisation and division of labour for producing more goods with less effort, and low costs

      (iii) vast capital

      (iv) large organizations

      (v) executive bureaucracy.

   * *Uneven Geographic Distribution* - Major concentrations of modern manufacturing have flourished in a few numbers of places. These cover less than 10 per cent of the world's land area. These nations have become the centres of economic and political power. However, in terms of the total area covered, manufacturing sites are much less conspicuous and concentrated on much smaller areas than that of agriculture due to greater intensity of processes. Industries maximise profits by reducing costs. Therefore, industries should be located at points where the production costs are minimum. Some of the factors influencing industrial locations are as under:

      ➢ *Access to Market:* The existence of a market for manufactured goods is the most important factor in the location of industries. 'Market' means people who have a demand for these goods and also have the purchasing power (ability to purchase) to be able to purchase from the sellers at a place. Remote areas inhabited by a few people offer small markets. The developed regions of Europe, North America, Japan and Australia provide large global markets as the purchasing power of the people is very high. The densely populated regions of South and South-east Asia also provide large markets. Some industries, such as aircraft manufacturing, have a global market. The arms industry also has global markets.

➢ *Access to Raw Material:* Raw material used by industries should be cheap and easy to transport. Industries based on cheap, bulky and weight-losing material (ores) are located close to the sources of raw material such as steel, sugar, and cement industries. Perishability is a vital factor for the industry to be located closer to the source of the raw material. Agro-processing and dairy products are processed close to the sources of farm produce or milk supply respectively.

➢ *Access to Labour Supply:* Labour supply is an important factor in the location of industries. Some types of manufacturing still require skilled labour. Increasing mechanisation, automation and flexibility of industrial processes have reduced the dependence of industry upon the labours.

➢ *Access to Sources of Energy:* Industries which use more power are located close to the source of the energy supply such as the aluminium industry. Earlier coal was the main source of energy; today hydroelectricity and petroleum are also important sources of energy for many industries.

➢ *Access to Transportation and Communication Facilities:* Speedy and efficient transport facilities to carry raw materials to the factory and to move finished goods to the market are essential for the development of industries. The cost of transport plays an important role in the location of industrial units. Western Europe and eastern North America have a highly developed transport system which has always induced the concentration of industries in these areas. Modern industry is inseparably tied to transportation systems. Improvements in transportation led to integrated economic development and regional specialisation of manufacturing. Communication is also an important need for industries for the exchange and management of information.

➢ *Government Policy:* Governments adopt 'regional policies' to promote 'balanced' economic development and hence set up industries in particular areas.

➢ *Access to Agglomeration Economies/ Links between Industries:* Many industries benefit from nearness to a leader-industry and other industries. These benefits are termed as agglomeration economies. Savings are derived from the linkages which exist between different industries.

❖ **Classification of Manufacturing Industries -** Manufacturing industries are classified on the basis of their size, inputs/raw materials, output/products and ownership.

● *Industries based on Size -* The amount of capital invested, number of workers employed and volume of production determine the size of industry. Accordingly, industries may be classified into household or cottage, small-scale and large-scale.

➢ Household Industries or Cottage Manufacturing: It is the smallest manufacturing unit. The artisans use local raw materials and simple tools to produce everyday goods in their homes with the help of their family members or part time labour. Finished products may be for consumption in the same household or, for sale in local (village) markets, or, for barter. Capital and transportation do not wield much influence as this type of manufacturing has low commercial significance and most of the tools are devised locally. Some common everyday products produced in this sector of manufacturing include foodstuffs, fabrics, mats, containers, tools, furniture, shoes, and figurines from wood lot and forest, shoes, thongs and other articles from leather; pottery and bricks from clays and stones. Goldsmiths make jewellery of gold, silver and bronze. Some artefacts and crafts are made out of bamboo, wood obtained locally from the forests.

➢ Small Scale Manufacturing: Small scale manufacturing is distinguished from household industries by its production techniques and place of manufacture (a workshop outside the home/cottage of the producer). This type of manufacturing uses local raw material, simple power-driven machines and semi-skilled labour. It provides employment and raises local purchasing power. Therefore, countries like India, China, Indonesia and Brazil, etc. have developed labour-intensive small scale manufacturing in order to provide employment to their population.

➢ Large Scale Manufacturing: Large scale manufacturing involves a large market, various raw materials, enormous energy, specialised workers, advanced technology, assembly-line mass production and large capital. This kind of manufacturing developed in the last 200 years, in the United Kingdom, north-eastern U.S.A. and Europe. Now it has diffused to almost all over the world. On the basis of the system of large scale manufacturing, the world's major industrial regions may be grouped under two broad types, namely (i) traditional large-scale industrial regions which are thickly clustered in a few more developed countries. (ii) high-technology large scale industrial regions which have diffused to less developed countries.

- Industries based on Inputs/Raw Materials - On the basis of the raw materials used, the industries are classified as: (a) agro-based; (b) mineral based; (c) chemical based; (d) forest based: and (e) animal based.

  (a) *Agro based Industries:* Agro processing involves the processing of raw materials from the field and the farm into finished products for rural and urban markets. Major agro-processing industries are food processing, sugar, pickles, fruits juices, beverages (tea, coffee and cocoa), spices and oils fats and textiles (cotton, jute, silk), rubber, etc.

    - *Food Processing:* Agro processing includes canning, producing cream, fruit processing and confectionery. While some preserving techniques, such as drying, fermenting and pickling, have been known since ancient times, these had limited applications to cater to the pre-Industrial Revolution demands.

  (b) *Mineral based Industries:* These industries use minerals as a raw material. Some industries use ferrous metallic minerals which contain ferrous (iron), such as iron and steel industries but some use non-ferrous metallic minerals, such as aluminium, copper and jewellery industries. Many industries use non-metallic minerals such as cement and pottery industries.

  (c) *Chemical based Industries:* Such industries use natural chemical minerals, e.g. mineral-oil (pctroleum) is used in petrochemical industry. Salts, sulphur and potash industries also use natural minerals. Chemical industries are also based on raw materials obtained from wood and coal. Synthetic fibre, plastic, etc. are other examples of chemical based industries.

  (d) *Forest based Raw Material using Industries:* The forests provide many major and minor products which are used as raw material. Timber for furniture industry, wood, bamboo and grass for paper industry, lac for lac industries come from forests.

  (e) *Animal based Industries:* Leather for leather industry and wool for woollen textiles are obtained from animals. Besides, ivory is also obtained from elephant's tusks.

- Industries Based On Output/Product - The industry whose products are used to make other goods by using them as raw materials are basic industries. The consumer goods industries produced goods which are consumed by consumers directly. For example, industries producing breads and biscuits, tea, soaps and toiletries, paper for writing, televisions, etc. are consumer goods or non-basic industries.

- Industries Based on Ownership –

  (a) Public Sector Industries are owned and managed by governments. In India, there were a number of Public Sector Undertakings (PSUs). Socialist countries have many state owned industries. Mixed economies have both Public and Private sector enterprises.

  (b) Private Sector Industries are owned by individual investors. These are managed by private organisations. In capitalist countries, industries are generally owned privately.

  (c) Joint Sector Industries are managed by joint stock companies or sometimes the private and public sectors together establish and manage the industries.

❖ Traditional Large-Scale Industrial Regions - These are based on heavy industry, often located near coal-fields and engaged in metal smelting, heavy engineering, chemical manufacture or textile production. These industries are now known as smokestack industries. Traditional industrial regions can be recognised by:

- High proportion of employment in manufacturing industry. High-density housing, often of inferior type, and poor services. Unattractive environment, for example, pollution, waste heaps, and so on.

- Problems of unemployment, emigration and derelict land areas caused by closure of factories because of a worldwide fall in demand.

❖ The Ruhr Coal-field, Germany - This has been one of the major industrial regions of Europe for a long time. Coal and iron and steel formed the basis of the economy, but as the demand for coal declined, the industry started shrinking. Even after the iron ore was exhausted, the industry remained, using imported ore brought by waterways to the Ruhr. The Ruhr region is responsible for 80 per cent of Germany's total steel production.

❖ Iron and Steel Industry - The iron and steel industry forms the base of all other industries and, therefore, it is called a basic industry. It is basic because it provides raw material for other industries such as machine tools used for further production. It may also be called a heavy industry because it uses large quantities of bulky raw materials and its products are also heavy. Iron is extracted from iron ore by smelting in a blast furnace with carbon (coke) and limestone. The molten iron is cooled and moulded to form pig iron which is used for converting into steel by adding strengthening materials like manganese. The large integrated steel industry is traditionally located close to the sources of raw materials – iron ore, coal, manganese and limestone – or at places where these could be easily brought, e.g. near ports. But in mini steel mills access to markets is more important than inputs. These are less expensive to build and operate and can be located near markets because of the abundance of scrap metal, which is the main input. Traditionally, most of the steel was produced at large integrated plants, but mini mills are limited to just one-step process – steel making – and are gaining ground. *Distribution*: The industry is one of the most complex and capital-intensive industries and is concentrated in the advanced countries of North America, Europe and Asia. In U.S.A, most of the production comes from the north Appalachian region (Pittsburgh), Great Lake region (Chicago-Gary, Erie, Cleveland, Lorain, Buffalo and Duluth) and the Atlantic Coast (Sparrows Point and Morisville). The industry has also moved towards the southern state of Alabama. Pittsburg area is now losing ground. It has now become the "rust bowl" of U.S.A. In Europe, U.K., Germany, France, Belgium, Luxembourgh, the Netherlands and Russia are the leading producers. The important steel centres are Scun Thorpe, Port Talbot, Birmingham and Sheffield in the U.K.; Duisburg, Dortmund, Dusseldorf and Essen in Germany; Le Creusot and St. Ettienne in France; and Moscow, St. Petersburgh, Lipetsk, Tula, in Russia and Krivoi Rog, and Donetsk in Ukraine. In Asia, the important centres include Nagasaki and Tokyo-Yokohama in Japan; Shanghai, Tienstin and Wuhan in China; and Jamshedpur, Kulti-Burnpur, Durgapur, Rourkela, Bhilai, Bokaro, Salem, Visakhapatnam and Bhadravati in India. Consult your atlas to locate these places/ centres.

❖ Cotton Textile Industry - Cotton textile industry has three sub-sectors i.e. handloom, powerloom and mill sectors. Handloom sector is labour-intensive and provides employment to semi-skilled workers. It requires small capital investment. This sector involves spinning, weaving and finishing of the fabrics. The powerloom sector introduces machines and becomes less labour intensive and the volume of production increases. Cotton textile mill sector is highly capital intensive and produces fine clothes in bulk. Cotton textile manufacturing requires good quality cotton as raw material. India, China, U.S.A, Pakistan, Uzbekistan, Egypt produce more than half of the world's raw cotton. The U.K, NW European countries and Japan also produce cotton textile made from imported yarn. Europe alone accounts for nearly half of the world's cotton imports. The industry has to face very stiff competition with synthetic fibres hence it has now shown a declining trend in many countries. With the scientific advancement and technological improvements the structure of industries changes.

❖ Concept of High Technology Industry - High technology, or simply high-tech, is the latest generation of manufacturing activities. It is best understood as the application of intensive research and development (R and D) efforts leading to the manufacture of products of an advanced scientific and engineering character. Professional (white collar) workers make up a large share of the total workforce. These highly skilled specialists greatly outnumber the actual production (blue collar) workers. Robotics on the assembly line, computer-aided design (CAD) and manufacturing, electronic controls of smelting and refining processes, and the constant development of new chemical and pharmaceutical products are notable examples of a high-tech industry. Neatly spaced, low, modern, dispersed, office-plant-lab buildings rather than massive assembly structures, factories and storage areas mark the high-tech industrial landscape. Planned business parks for high-tech start-ups have become part of regional and local development schemes. High-tech industries which are regionally concentrated, self-sustained and highly specialised are called technopolies. The Silicon Valley near San Francisco and Silicon Forest near Seattle are examples of technopolies.

Exercise

1. _________ activities add value to natural resources by *transforming* raw materials into valuable products.
   - (a) Primary
   - (b) Secondary
   - (c) Tertiary
   - (d) Quaternary

2. _________ involves a full array of production from handicrafts to moulding iron and steel and stamping out plastic toys to assembling delicate computer components or space vehicles.
   - (a) Manufacturing
   - (b) Processing
   - (c) Construction
   - (d) Infrastructure

3. Under the '--------_________' method factories produce only a few pieces which are made-to-order.
   - (a) Mass
   - (b) Whole
   - (c) Craft
   - (d) Production

4. _________ refers to using gadgets which accomplish tasks.
   - (a) Mechanisation
   - (b) Automation
   - (c) Technological Innovation
   - (d) Manufacturing

5. The existence of a _________ for manufactured goods is the most important factor in the location of industries.
   - (a) Capital
   - (b) Market
   - (c) Money
   - (d) Goods

6. Which one of the following statements is NOT correct?
   - (a) Cheap water transport has facilitated the jute mill industry along the Hugli.
   - (b) Sugar, cotton textiles and vegetable oils are footloose industries.
   - (c) The development of hydro-electricity and petroleum reduced, to a great extent, the importance of coal energy as a locational factor for industry.
   - (d) Port towns in India have attracted industries.

7. In which one of the following types of economy are the factors of production owned individually?
   - (a) Capitalist
   - (b) Mixed
   - (c) Socialist
   - (d) None

8. Which one of the following types of industries produces raw materials for other industries?
   - (a) Cottage Industries
   - (b) Small-scale Industries
   - (c) Basic Industries
   - (d) Footloose Industries

9. The iron and steel industry forms the base of all other industries and, therefore, it is called a _________ industry.
   - (a) Basic
   - (b) Main
   - (c) Side
   - (d) Supporting

10. _____________ industry has three sub-sectors i.e. handloom, powerloom and mill sectors.
    - (a) Iron and Steel
    - (b) Cotton textile
    - (c) Mineral
    - (d) Agro

11. Which of the following industry is NOT an industry based on Ownership?
    - (a) Public Sector
    - (b) Mineral Based
    - (c) Private Sector
    - (d) Joint Sector

12. Consider the following statements:
    1. High-technology large scale industrial regions which are thickly clustered in a few more developed countries.
    2. Traditional large-scale industrial regions which have diffused to less developed countries.

    Which of the following statements is/are correct?
    - (a) 1 only
    - (b) 2 only
    - (c) Both 1 and 2
    - (d) Neither 1 nor 2

13. It is the smallest manufacturing unit. The artisans use local raw materials and simple tools to produce everyday goods in their homes with the help of their family members or parttime labour. Finished products may be for consumption in the same household or, for sale in local (village) markets, or, for barter. Capital and transportation do not wield much influence as this type of manufacturing has low commercial significance and most of the tools are devised locally.

    Above given statement defines which of the following industry?
    - (a) Household Industries or Cottage Manufacturing
    - (b) Small Scale Manufacturing
    - (c) Large Scale Manufacturing
    - (d) Agro based Industries

14. Consider the following statements about a Foot Loose Industry:
    1. They are dependent on any specific raw material, weight losing or otherwise.
    2. They largely depend on component parts which can be obtained anywhere.

3. They produce in small quantity and also employ a small labour force.

4. These are generally polluting industries.

5. The important factor in their location is accessibility by road network.

Which of the above given statements are correct?

(a) 1 and 4 only   (b) 2, 3 and 5 only

(c) 2 and 4 only   (d) 1, 2, 3, 4 and 5

15. Which of the following factors are influencing industrial locations?

1. Access to Market

2. Access to Raw Material

3. Access to Labour Supply

4. Access to Source of Energy

5. Access to Transportation and Communication Facilities

6. Government policy

Select the correct answer using the code given below:

(a) 1, 3 and 5 only   (b) 2, 4 and 6 only

(c) 1, 2, 3, 4 and 5 only   (d) 1, 2, 3, 4, 5 and 6

16. Consider the following pairs:

1. Automobile industry.... Los Angeles

2. Shipbuilding industry.... Lusaka

3. Aircraft industry.... Florence

4. Iron and Steel industry.... Pittsburgh

Which of the above given pairs is/are correctly matched?

(a) 1 and 4 only   (b) 2 and 3 only

(c) 4 only   (d) 2 and 4 only

17. Assertion: Therefore, industries should be located at points where the production costs are minimum.

Reasoning: Industries maximise profits by reducing costs.

(a) Both the Assertion and the Reason are correct and the Reason is the correct explanation of the Assertion.

(b) Both the Assertion and the Reason are correct but the Reason is not the correct explanation of the Assertion.

(c) The Assertion is incorrect but the Reason is correct.

(d) The Assertion is correct but the Reason is incorrect.

18. Modern manufacturing is characterised by -

1. a complex machine technology

2. extreme specialisation and division of labour for producing more goods with less effort, and low costs

3. vast capital

4. large organisations

5. executive bureaucracy

Select the correct answer using the code given below:

(a) 2, 4 and 5 only   (b) 1, 3 and 5 only

(c) 2, 3, 4 and 5 only   (d) 1, 2, 3, 4 and 5

19. Consider the following statements:

1. Manufacturing literally means *'to make by hand'*. However, now it includes goods 'made by machines'.

2. It is essentially a process which involves *transforming raw materials into finished goods of higher value for sale in local or distant markets.*

Which of the following statements is/are correct?

(a) 1 only   (b) 2 only

(c) Both 1 and 2   (d) Neither 1 nor 2

20. Secondary activities are concerned with which of the following industries?

1. Manufacturing

2. Processing

3. Construction

Select the correct answer using the code give below:

(a) 1 and 2 only   (b) 1 and 3 only

(c) 2 and 3 only   (d) 1, 2 and 3

Answers

1. (b)	2. (a)	3. (c)	4. (a)	5. (b)	6. (b)	7. (a)	8. (c)	9. (a)	10. (b)
11. (b)	12. (d)	13. (a)	14. (b)	15. (d)	16. (c)	17. (a)	18. (d)	19. (c)	20. (d)

Tertiary and Quaternary Activities

* Tertiary activities are related to the service sector. Manpower is an important component of the service sector as most of the tertiary activities are performed by skilled labour, professionally trained experts and consultants.

* In the initial stages of economic development, larger proportion of people worked in the primary sector. In a developed economy, the majority of workers get employment in tertiary activity and a moderate proportion is employed in the secondary sector.

* Tertiary activities include both production and exchange. The production involves the 'provision' of services that are 'consumed'. The output is indirectly measured in terms of wages and salaries. Exchange, involves trade, transport and communication facilities that are used to overcome distance. Tertiary activities, therefore, involve the commercial output of services rather than the production of tangible goods. They are not directly involved in the processing of physical raw materials.

* The main difference between secondary activities and tertiary activities is that the expertise provided by services relies more heavily on specialised skills, experience and knowledge of the workers rather than on the production techniques, machinery and factory processes.

* Types of Tertiary Activities: Trade, transport, communication and services are some of the tertiary activities.

* Trade and commerce - Trade is essentially buying and selling of items produced elsewhere. All the services in retail and wholesale trading or commerce are specifically intended for profit. The towns and cities where all these works take place are known us trading centres. The rise of trading from barter at the local level to money-exchange of international scale has produced many centres and institutions such as trading centres or collection and distribution points. Trading centres may be divided into rural and urban marketing centres. *Rural marketing centres* cater to nearby settlements. These are quasi-urban centres. They serve as trading centres of the most rudimentary type. Here personal and professional services are not well-developed. These form local collecting and distributing centres. Most of these have *mandis* (wholesale markets) and also retailing areas. They are not urban centres *per se* but are significant centres for making available goods and services which are most frequently demanded by rural folk. *Periodic markets in rural areas* are found where there are no regular markets and local periodic markets are organised at different temporal intervals. These may be weekly, biweekly markets from where people from the surrounding areas meet their temporally accumulated demand. These markets are held on specified dates and move from one place to another. The shopkeepers thus, remain busy on all the days while a large area is served by them. *Urban marketing centres* have more widely specialised urban services. They provide ordinary goods and services as well as many of the specialised goods and services required by people. Urban centres, therefore, offer manufactured goods as well as many specialised markets develop, e.g. markets for labour, housing, seml or finished products. Services of educational institutions and professionals such as teachers, lawyers, consultants, physicians, dentists and veterinary doctors are available.

* *Retail Trading:* This is the business activity concerned with the sale of goods directly to the consumers. Most of the retail trading takes place in fixed establishments or stores solely devoted to selling. Street peddling, handcarts, trucks, door-to-door, mail-order, telephone, automatic vending machines and internet are examples of non-store retail trading.

❖ *Wholesale Trading:* Wholesale trading constitutes bulk business through numerous intermediary merchants and supply houses and not through retail stores. Some large stores including chain stores are able to buy directly from the manufacturers. However, most retail stores procure supplies from an intermediary source. Wholesalers often extend credit to retail stores to such an extent that the retailer operates very largely on the wholesaler's capital.

❖ Transport - Transport is a service or facility by which people, materials and manufactured goods are physically carried from one location to another. It is an organised industry created to satisfy man's basic need of mobility. Modern society requires speedy and efficient transport systems to assist in the production, distribution and consumption of goods. At every stage in this complex system, the value of the material is significantly enhanced by transportation. Transport distance can be measured as: km distance or actual distance of route length; time distance or the time taken to travel on a particular route; and cost distance or the expense of travelling on a route. In selecting the mode of transport, distance, in terms of time or cost, is the determining factor. Isochrone lines are drawn on a map to join places equal in terms of the time taken to reach them. *Factors Affecting Transport:* Demand for transport is influenced by the size of population. The larger the population size, the greater is the demand for transport. Routes depend on: location of cities, towns, villages, industrial centres and raw materials, pattern of trade between them, nature of the landscape between them, type of climate, and funds available for overcoming obstacles along the length of the route.

❖ Communication - Communication services involve the transmission of words and messages, facts and ideas. The invention of writing preserved messages and helped to make communication dependent on means of transport. These were actually carried by hand, animals, boat, road, rail and air. That is why all forms of transport are also referred to as lines of communication.

❖ *Telecommunications:* The use of telecommunications is linked to the development of modern technology. It has revolutionised communications because of the speed with which messages are sent. The time reduced is from weeks to minutes. Besides, the recent advancements like mobile telephony have made communications direct and instantaneous at any time and from anywhere.

❖ Services - Professional services are primarily health care, engineering, law and management. The location of recreational and entertainment services depends on the market. Multiplexes and restaurants might find location within or near the Central Business District (CBD), whereas a golf course would choose a site where land costs are lower than in the CBD.

❖ *Tourism* - Tourism is travel undertaken for purposes of recreation rather than business. It has become the world's single largest tertiary activity in total registered jobs (250 million) and total revenue (40 per cent of the total GDP). Besides, many local persons are employed to provide services like accommodation, meals, transport, entertainment and special shops serving the tourists. Tourism fosters the growth of infrastructure industries, retail trading, and craft industries (souvenirs). In some regions, tourism is seasonal because the vacation period is dependent on favourable weather conditions, but many regions attract visitors all the year round.

❖ *Tourist Regions:* The warmer places around the Mediterranean Coast and the West Coast of India are some of the popular tourist destinations in the world. Others include winter sports regions, found mainly in mountainous areas, and various scenic landscapes and national parks, which are scattered. Historic towns also attract tourists, because of the monument, heritage sites and cultural activities.

❖ *Factors Affecting Tourism:*

Demand: Since the last century, the demand for holidays has increased rapidly. Improvements in the standard of living and increased leisure time permit many more people to go on holidays for leisure.

Transport: The opening-up of tourist areas has been aided by improvement in transport facilities.

❖ Medical Services for Overseas Patients in India - About 55,000 patients from U.S.A. visited India in 2005 for treatment. This is still a small number compared with the millions of surgeries performed each year in the U.S. healthcare system. India has emerged as the leading country of medical tourism in the world. World class hospitals located in metropolitan cities cater to patients all over the world. Medical tourism brings abundant benefits to developing countries like India, Thailand, Singapore and Malaysia. Beyond medical tourism, is the trend of outsourcing of medical tests and data interpretation. Hospitals in India, Switzerland and

Australia have been performing certain medical services – ranging from reading radiology images, to interpreting Magnetic Resonance Images (MRIs) and ultrasound tests. Outsourcing holds tremendous advantages for patients, if it is focused on improving quality or providing specialised care.

❖ Quaternary activities involve some of the following: the collection, production and dissemination of information or even the production of information. Quaternary activities centre around research, development and may be seen as an advanced form of services involving specialised knowledge and technical skills.

❖ Quinary Activities - The highest level of decision makers or policy makers perform quinary activities. These are subtly different from the knowledge based industries that the quinary sector in general deals with. Outsourcing has resulted in the opening up of a large number of call centres in India, China, Eastern Europe, Israel, Philippines and Costa Rica. It has created new jobs in these countries. Outsourcing is coming to those countries where cheap and skilled workers are available. New trends in quinary services include knowledge processing outsourcing (KPO) and 'home shoring', the latter as an alternative to outsourcing. The KPO industry is distinct from Business Process Outsourcing (BPO) as it involves highly skilled workers. It is information driven knowledge outsourcing. KPO enables companies to create additional business opportunities. Examples of KPOs include research and development (R and D) activities, e-learning, business research, intellectual property (IP) research, legal profession and the banking sector.

❖ The Digital Divide - Opportunities emerging from the Information and Communication Technology based development is unevenly distributed across the globe. There are wide ranging economic, political and social differences among countries. How quickly countries can provide ICT access and benefits to its citizens are the deciding factor. While developed countries in general have surged forward, the developing countries have lagged behind and this is known as the digital divide. Similarly digital divides exist within countries.

Exercise

1. Which one of the following is a tertiary activity?
   - (a) Farming
   - (b) Trading
   - (c) Weaving
   - (d) Hunting

2. Which one of the following activities is NOT a secondary sector activity?
   - (a) Iron Smelting
   - (b) Catching fish
   - (c) Making garments
   - (d) Basket Weaving

3. Which one of the following sector provides most of the employment in Delhi, Mumbai, Chennai and Kolkata?
   - (a) Primary
   - (b) Quaternary
   - (c) Secondary
   - (d) Service

4. Jobs that involve high degrees and level of innovations are known as:
   - (a) Secondary activities
   - (b) Quaternary activities
   - (c) Quinary activities
   - (d) Primary activities

5. Which one of the following activities is related to quaternary sector?
   - (a) Manufacturing computers
   - (b) Paper and Raw pulp production
   - (c) University teaching
   - (d) Printing books

6. Which one out of the following statements is NOT correct?
   - (a) Outsourcing reduces costs and increases efficiency.
   - (b) At times engineering and manufacturing jobs can also be outsourced.
   - (c) BPOs have better business opportunities as compared to KPOs.
   - (d) There may be dissatisfaction among job seekers in the countries that outsource the job.

7. Tertiary activities include both production and __________.
   - (a) Exchange
   - (b) Transportation
   - (c) Manufacturing
   - (d) Packaging

8. Street peddling, handcarts, trucks, door-to-door, mail-order, telephone, automatic vending machines and internet are examples of ____________ retail trading.
   - (a) store
   - (b) non-store
   - (c) market
   - (d) non-market

9. 'Gold collar' profession is related to which of the following activities?
   - (a) Tertiary
   - (b) Secondary
   - (c) Quinary
   - (d) Quaternary

10. A __________ is the meeting point of two or more routes, a point of origin, a point of destination or any sizeable town along a route.
    - (a) Node
    - (b) Link
    - (c) Network
    - (d) Point

11. CBD stands for –
    - (a) Central Business Division
    - (b) Central Business Direction
    - (c) Central Business Divide
    - (d) Central Business District

12. Which of the following sector is also known as 'knowledge sector'?
    - (a) Primary
    - (b) Secondary
    - (c) Tertiary
    - (d) Quaternary

13. It has become the world's single largest tertiary activity in total registered jobs (250 million) and total revenue (40 per cent of the total GDP). Besides, many local persons are employed to provide services like accommodation, meals, transport, entertainment and special shops serving the tourists.

    Above paragraph defines which of the following activities?
    - (a) Tourism
    - (b) Medical services
    - (c) Transport
    - (d) Telecommunication

14. Opportunities emerging from the Information and Communication Technology based development is unevenly distributed across the globe. There are wide ranging economic, political and social differences among countries. How quickly countries can provide ICT access and benefits to its citizens are the deciding factor. While developed countries in general have surged forward, the developing countries have lagged behind and this is known as the __________.
    - (a) digital divide
    - (b) digital gap
    - (c) digital lag
    - (d) digital difference

15. Consider the following pairs:
    1. Chain stores: delegate the responsibility and authority to departmental heads for purchasing of commodities and for overseeing the sale in different sections of the stores.
    2. Departmental stores: are able to purchase merchandise most economically, often going so far as to direct the goods to be manufactured to their specification. They employ highly skilled specialists in many executive tasks. They have the ability to experiment in one store and apply the results to many.

Which of the above given pairs are correctly matched?

(a) 1 only   (b) 2 only

(c) Both 1 and 2   (d) Neither 1 nor 2

16. Assertion: This is the business activity concerned with the sale of goods directly to the consumers.

Reasoning: Most of the retail trading takes place in fixed establishments or stores solely devoted to selling.

(a) Both the Assertion and the Reason are correct and the Reason is the correct explanation of the Assertion.

(b) Both the Assertion and the Reason are correct but the Reason is not the correct explanation of the Assertion.

(c) The Assertion is incorrect but the Reason is correct.

(d) The Assertion is correct but the Reason is incorrect.

17. Consider the following statements:

1. Rural marketing centres cater to nearby settlements. These are quasi-urban centres.

2. They serve as trading centres of the most rudimentary type.

3. Here personal and professional services are not well-developed.

4. These form local collecting and distributing centres. Most of these have mandis (wholesale markets) and also retailing areas.

Which of the following statements are correct?

(a) 1 and 2 only   (b) 2 and 3 only

(c) 1, 2 and 3 only   (d) 1, 2, 3 and 4

18. Consider the following statements:

1. Trade is essentially only buying of items produced elsewhere.

2. All the services in retail and wholesale trading or commerce are specifically intended for profit.

3. The towns and cities where all these works take place are known us trading centres.

Which of the statements given above are correct?

(a) 1 and 2 only   (b) 1 and 3 only

(c) 2 and 3 only   (d) 1, 2 and 3

19. These have more widely specialised urban services. They provide ordinary goods and services as well as many of the specialised goods and services required by people. Urban centres, therefore, offer manufactured goods as well as many specialised markets develop, e.g. markets for labour, housing, semi or finished products. Services of educational institutions and professionals such as teachers, lawyers, consultants, physicians, dentists and veterinary doctors are available.

Above paragraph defines which of the following market?

(a) Rural marketing centres

(b) Urban marketing centres

(c) Periodic marketing centres

(d) Central marketing centres

20. Consider the following statements about Periodic Markets:

1. Periodic markets in rural areas are found where there are no regular markets and local periodic markets are organised at different temporal intervals.

2. These may be weekly, bi-weekly markets from where people from the surrounding areas meet their temporally accumulated demand.

3. These markets are held on any date and not move from one place to another.

4. The shopkeepers thus, remain busy on all the days while a large area is served by them.

Which of the statements given above are correct?

(a) 1 and 4 only

(b) 2 and 3 only

(c) 1, 2 and 3 only

(d) 1, 2 and 4 only

Answers

1. (b)	**2.** (b)	**3.** (d)	**4.** (c)	**5.** (c)	**6.** (c)	**7.** (a)	**8.** (b)	**9.** (c)	**10.** (a)
11. (d)	**12.** (d)	**13.** (a)	**14.** (a)	**15.** (d)	**16.** (b)	**17.** (d)	**18.** (c)	**19.** (b)	**20.** (d)

Your Notes :

Transport and Communication

- Transport is a service or facility for the carriage of persons and goods from one place to the other using humans, animals and different kinds of vehicles. Such movements take place over land, water and air. Roads and railways form part of land transport; while shipping and waterways and airways are the other two modes. Pipelines carry materials like petroleum, natural gas, and ores in liquidified form. Moreover, transportation is an organized service industry created to satisfy the basic needs of society. It includes transport arteries, vehicles to carry people and goods, and the organisation to maintain arteries, and to handle loading, unloading and delivery. Every nation has developed various kinds of transportation for defence purposes. Assured and speedy transportation, along with efficient communication, promote cooperation and unity among scattered peoples.

- Modes of Transportation - The principal modes of world transportation, as already mentioned are land, water, air and pipelines. These are used for inter-regional and intra-regional transport, and each one (except pipelines) carries both passengers and freight. The significance of a mode depends on the type of goods and services to be transported, costs of transport and the mode available.

- Land Transport - Most of the movement of goods and services takes place over land. In early days, humans themselves were carriers. Later animals were used as beasts of burden. With the invention of the wheel, the use of carts and wagons became important. The revolution in transport came about only after the invention of the steam engine in the eighteenth century. Perhaps the first public railway line was opened in 1825 between Stockton and Darlington in northern England and then onwards, railways became the most popular and fastest form of transport in the nineteenth century. It opened up continental interiors for commercial grain farming, mining and manufacturing in U.S.A. The invention of the internal combustion engine revolutionised road transport in terms of road quality and vehicles (motor cars and trucks) plying over them. Among the newer developments in land transportation are pipelines, ropeways and cableways. Liquids like mineral oil, water, sludge and sewers are transported by pipelines. The great freight carriers are the railways, ocean vessels, barges, boats and motor trucks and pipelines.

- Roads - Road transport is the most economical for short distances compared to railways. Freight transport by road is gaining importance because it offers door-to-door service. But unmetalled roads, though simple in construction, are not effective and serviceable for all seasons. During the rainy season these become unmotorable and even the metalled ones are seriously handicapped during heavy rains and floods. In such conditions, the high embankment of rail-tracks and the efficient maintenance of railway transport service is an effective solution. In developed countries good quality roads are universal and provide long-distance links in the form of motorways, autobahns (Germany), and inter–state highways for speedy movement. Lorries, of increasing size and power to carry heavy loads, are common. The world's total motorable road length is only about 15 million km, of which North America accounts for 33 per cent. The highest road density and the highest number of vehicles are registered in this continent compared to Western Europe.

- Traffic Flows: Traffic on roads has increased dramatically in recent years. When the road network cannot cope with the demands of traffic, congestion occurs. City roads suffer from chronic traffic congestion.

- Highways - Highways are metalled roads connecting distant places. They are constructed in a manner for unobstructed vehicular movement. As such these are 80 m wide, with separate traffic lanes, bridges, flyovers and dual carriageways to facilitate uninterrupted traffic flow. In developed countries, every city and port town is linked through highways. In North America, highway density is high, about 0.65 km per sq km. Every place is within 20 km distance from a highway. Cities located on the Pacific coast (west) are well-connected with those of the Atlantic Coast (east). Likewise, the cities of Canada in the north are linked with those of Mexico in the south. The Trans-Canadian Highway links Vancouver in British Columbia (west coast) to St. John's City in Newfoundland (east coast) and the

Alaskan Highway links Edmonton (Canada) to Anchorage (Alaska). The Pan-American Highway, a large portion of which has been constructed, will connect the countries of South America, Central America and U.S.A.-Canada. The Trans- Continental Stuart Highway connects Darwin (north coast) and Melbourne via Tennant Creek and Alice Springs in Australia. Europe has a large number of vehicles and a well-developed highway network. In Russia, a dense highway network is developed in the industrialised region west of the Urals with Moscow as the hub. The important Moscow-Vladivostok Highway serves the region to the east. In China, highways criss-cross the country connecting all major cities such as Tsungtso (near Vietnam boundary), Shanghai (central China), Guangzhou (south) and Beijing (north). A new highway links Chengdu with Lhasa in Tibet. In India, there are many highways linking the major towns and cities. For example, National Highway No. 7 (NH 7), connecting Varanasi with Kanya Kumari, is the longest in the country. The Golden Quadrilateral (GQ) or Super Expressway is underway to connect the four metropolitan cities — New Delhi, Mumbai, Bangalore, Chennai, Kolkata and Hyderabad. In Africa, a highway joins Algiers in the north to Conakry in Guinea. Similarly, Cairo is also connected to Cape Town.

❖ Border Roads - Roads laid along international boundaries are called border roads. They play an important role in integrating people in remote areas with major cities and providing defence. Almost all countries have such roads to transport goods to border villages and military camps.

❖ Railways - Railways are a mode of land transport for bulky goods and passengers over long distances. The railway gauges vary in different countries and are roughly classified as broad (more than 1.5 m), standard (1.44 m), metre gauge (1 m) and smaller gauges. The standard gauge is used in the U.K. Commuter trains are very popular in U.K., U.S.A, Japan and India. These carry millions of passengers daily to and fro in the city. There is about 13 lakh km of railways open for traffic in the world. Europe has one of the most dense rail networks in the world. There are about 4,40,000 km of railways, most of which is double or multiple-tracked. Belgium has the highest density of 1 km of railway for every 6.5 sq kms area. The industrial regions exhibit some of the highest densities in the world. The important rail heads are London, Paris, Brussels, Milan, Berlin and Warsaw. Underground railways are important in London and Paris. Channel Tunnel, operated by Euro Tunnel Group through England, connects London with Paris. In Russia, railways account for about 90 per cent of the country's total transport with a very dense network west of the Urals. North America has one of the most extensive rail networks accounting for nearly 40 per cent of the world's total? In contrast to many European countries, the railways are used more for long-distance bulky freight like ores, grains, timber and machinery than for passengers. The most dense rail network is found in the highly industrialised and urbanised region of East Central U.S.A. and adjoining Canada. In Canada, railways are in the public sector and distributed all over the sparsely populated areas. The transcontinental railways carry the bulk of wheat and coal tonnage. Australia has about 40,000 km of railways, of which 25 per cent are found in New South Wales alone. The west-east Australian National Railway line runs across the country from Perth to Sydney. New Zealand's railways are mainly in the North Island to serve the farming areas. In South America, the rail network is the most dense in two regions, namely, the Pampas of Argentina and the coffee growing region of Brazil which together account for 40 per cent of South America's total route length. There is only one trans-continental rail route linking Buenos Aires (Argentina) with Valparaiso (Chile) across the Andes Mountains through the Uspallatta Pass located at a height of 3,900 m. In Asia, rail network is the densest in the thickly populated areas of Japan, China and India. West Asia is the least developed in rail facilities because of vast deserts and sparsely populated regions. Africa continent, despite being the second largest, has only 40,000 km of railways with South Africa alone accounting for 18,000 km due to the concentration of gold, diamond and copper mining activities. The important routes of the continent are: (i) the Benguela Railway through Angola to Katanga-Zambia Copper Belt; (ii) the Tanzania Railway from the Zambian Copper Belt to Dar-es-Salaam on the coast; (iii) the Railway through Botswana and Zimbabwe linking the landlocked states to the South African network; and (iv) the Blue Train from Cape Town to Pretoria in the Republic of South Africa.

❖ Trans–Continental Railways - Trans–continental railways run across the continent and link its two ends. They were constructed for economic and political reasons to facilitate long runs in different directions.

❖ Trans–Siberian Railway - This is a trans–siberian Railways major rail route of Russia runs from St. Petersburg in the west to Vladivostok on the Pacific Coast in the east passing through Moscow, Ufa, Novosibirsk, Irkutsk, Chita and Khabarovsk. It is the most important route in Asia and the longest (9,332 km) double-tracked and electrified trans–continental railway in the world. It has helped in opening up its Asian region to West European markets. It runs across the Ural Mountains Ob and Yenisei rivers Chita is an important agrocentre and Irkutsk, a fur centre.

There are connecting links to the south, namely, to Odessa (Ukraine), Baku on the Caspian Coast, Tashkent (Uzbekistan), Ulan Bator (Mongolia), and Shenyang (Mukden) and Beijing in China.

- Trans–Canadian Railways - This 7,050 km long rail-line in Canada runs from Halifax in the east to Vancouver on the Pacific Coast passing through Montreal, Ottawa, Winnipeg and Calgary. It was constructed in 1886, initially as part of an agreement to make British Columbia on the west coast join the Federation of States. Later on, it gained economic significance because it connected the Quebec-Montreal Industrial Region with the wheat belt of the Prairie Region and the Coniferous Forest region in the north. Thus each of these regions became complementary to the other. A loop line from Winnipeg to Thunder Bay (Lake Superior) connects this rail-line with one of the important waterways of the world. This line is the economic artery of Canada. Wheat and meat are the important exports on this route.

- The Union and Pacific Railway - This rail-line connects New York on the Atlantic Coast to San Francisco on the Pacific Coast passing through Cleveland, Chicago, Omaha, Evans, Ogden and Sacramento. The most valuable exports on this route are ores, grain, paper, chemicals and machinery.

- The Australian Trans–Continental Railway - This rail-line runs west-east across the southern part of the continent from Perth on the west coast, to Sydney on the east coast. Passing through Kalgoorlie, Broken Hill and Port Augusta. Another major north-south line connects Adelaide and Alice Spring and to be joined further to the Darwin–Birdum line.

- The Orient Express - This line runs from Paris to Istanbul passing through Strasbourg, Munich, Vienna, Budapest and Belgrade. The journey time from London to Istanbul by this Express is now reduced to 96 hours as against 10 days by the sea-route. The chief exports on this rail-route are cheese, bacon, oats, wine, fruits, and machinery. There is a proposal to build a Trans–Asiatic Railway linking Istanbul with Bangkok via Iran, Pakistan, India, Bangladesh and Myanmar.

- Water Transport - One of the great advantages of water transportation is that it does not require route construction. The oceans are linked with each other and are negotiable with ships of various sizes.

- *The Northern Atlantic Sea Route:* This links North-eastern U.S.A. and Northwestern Europe, the two industrially developed regions of the world. The foreign trade over this route is greater than that of the rest of the world combined. One fourth of the world's foreign trade moves on this route. It is, therefore, the busiest in the world and otherwise, called the Big Trunk Route.

- *The Mediterranean–Indian Ocean Sea Route:* This sea route passes through the heart of the Old World and serves more countries and people than any other route. Port Said, Aden, Mumbai, Colombo and Singapore are some of the important ports on this route. The construction of Suez Canal has greatly reduced the distance and time as compared to the earlier route through the Cape of Good Hope, which was longer than the route through Suez Canal.

- *The Cape of Good Hope Sea Route:* This trade route connects the highly industrialised Western European region with West Africa, South Africa, South-east Asia and the commercial agriculture and livestock economies of Australia and New Zealand. The volume of trade and traffic between both East and West Africa is on the increase due to the development of the rich natural resources such as gold, diamond, copper, tin, groundnut, oil palm, coffee and fruits.

- *The Southern Atlantic Sea Route:* This sea route is another important one across the Atlantic Ocean which connects West European and West African countries with Brazil, Argentina and Uruguay in South America.

- *The North Pacific Sea Route:* Trade across the vast North Pacific Ocean moves by several routes which converge at Honolulu. The direct route on the Great Circle links Vancouver and Yokohama and reduces the travelling distance (2,480 km) by half. This sea route links the ports on the westcoast of North America with those of Asia. These are Vancouver, Seattle, Portland, San Francisco and Los Angeles on the American side and Yokohama, Kobe, Shanghai, Hong Kong, Manila and Singapore on the Asian side.

- *The South Pacific Sea Route:* This sea route connects Western Europe and North America with Australia, New Zealand and the scattered Pacific islands via the Panama Canal. This route is also used for reaching Hong Kong, Philippines and Indonesia. The distance covered between Panama and Sydney is 12,000 km. Honolulu is an important port on this route.

- *The Suez Canal:* This canal had been constructed in 1869 in Egypt between Port Said in the north and Port Suez in the south linking the Mediterranean Sea and the Red Sea. It gives Europe a new gateway to the Indian Ocean and reduces direct sea-route distance between Liverpool and Colombo compared to the Cape of Good Hope route. It is a sea-level canal without locks which is about 160 km and 11 to 15 m deep. About 100 ships travel daily and each ship takes 10-12 hours to cross this canal. A railway follows the canal to Suez, and from Ismailia there is a branch line to Cairo. A navigable fresh-water canal from the Nile also joins the Suez Canal in Ismailia to supply fresh-water to Port Said and Suez.

❖ *The Panama Canal:* This canal connects the Atlantic Ocean in the east to the Pacific Ocean in the west. It has been constructed across the Panama Isthmus between Panama City and Colon by the U.S. government which purchased 8 km of area on either side and named it the Canal Zone. The Canal is about 72 km. long and involves a very deep cutting for a length of 12 km. It has a six-lock system and ships cross the different levels (26 m up and down) through these locks before entering the Gulf of Panama. It shortens the distance between New York and San Francisco by 13,000 km by sea. Likewise the distance between Western Europe and the West-coast of U.S.A.; and North-eastern and Central U.S.A. and East and South-east Asia is shortened.

❖ Inland Waterways - The development of inland waterways is dependent on the navigability width and depth of the channel, continuity in the water flow, and transport technology in use.

❖ The Rhine Waterways - The Rhine flows through Germany and the Netherlands. It is navigable for 700 km from Rotterdam, at its mouth in the Netherlands to Basel in Switzerland. Ocean-going vessels can reach up to Cologne. The Ruhr river joins the Rhine from the east. It flows through a rich coalfield and the whole basin has become a prosperous manufacturing area. Dusseldorf is the Rhine port for this region. Huge tonnage moves along the stretch south of the Ruhr. This waterway is the world's most heavily used. Each year more than 20,000 ocean-going ships and 2,00,000 inland vessels exchange their cargoes. It connects the industrial areas of Switzerland, Germany, France, Belgium and the Netherlands with the North Atlantic Sea Route.

❖ *The Danube Waterway:* This important inland waterway serves Eastern Europe. The Danube river rises in the Black Forest and flows eastwards through many countries. It is navigable up to Taurna Severin. The chief export items are wheat, maize, timber, and machinery.

❖ *The Volga Waterway:* Russia has a large number of developed waterways, of which the Volga is one of the most important. It provides a navigable waterway of 11,200 km and drains into the Caspian Sea. The Volga-Moscow Canal connects it with the Moscow region and the Volga-Don Canal with the Black Sea.

❖ *The Great Lakes – St. Lawrence Seaway:* The Great Lakes of North America Superior, Huron Erie and Ontario are connected by Soo Canal and Welland Canal to form an inland waterway. The estuary of St. Lawrence River, along with the Great Lakes, forms a unique commercial waterway in the northern part of North America.

❖ *The Mississippi Waterways:* The Mississippi-Ohio waterway connects the interior part of U.S.A. with the Gulf of Mexico in the south. Large steamers can go through this route up to Minneapolis.

❖ Inter-Continental Air Routes - In the Northern Hemisphere, there is a distinct east-west belt of inter-continental air routes. Dense network exists in Eastern U.S.A., Western Europe and Southeast Asia. U.S.A. alone accounts for 60 per cent of the airways of the world. New York, London, Paris, Amsterdam, Frankfurt Rome, Moscow, Karachi, New Delhi, Mumbai, Bangkok, Singapore, Tokyo, San Francisco, Los Angeles and Chicago are the nodal points where air routes converge or radiate to all continents.

❖ Pipelines - Pipelines are used extensively to transport liquids and gases such as water, petroleum and natural gas for an uninterrupted flow. In New Zealand, milk is being supplied through pipelines from farms to factories. In U.S.A. there is a dense network of oil pipelines from the producing areas to the consuming areas. Big Inch is one such famous pipeline, which carries petroleum from the oil wells of the Gulf of Mexico to the North-eastern States. About 17 per cent of all freight per tonne-km. is carried through pipelines in U.S.A. In Europe, Russia, West Asia and India pipelines are used to connect oil wells to refineries, and to ports or domestic markets. Turkmenistan is central Asia has extended pipelines to Iran and also to parts of China. The proposed Iran-India via Pakistan international oil and natural gas pipeline will be the longest in the world.

❖ Satellite Communication - Today Internet is the largest electronic network on the planet connecting about 1,000 million people in more than 100 countries. Communication through satellites emerged as a new area in communication technology since the 1970s after U.S.A. and former U.S.S.R. pioneered space research. India has also made great strides in satellite development. Aryabhatt was launched on 19 April 1979, Bhaskar-I in 1979 and Rohini in 1980. On 18 June 1981, APPLE (Arian Passenger Payload Experiment) was launched through Arian rocket. Bhaskar, Challenger and INSAT I-B have made longdistance communication, television and radio very effective.

❖ Cyber Space – Internet - Cyberspace is the world of electronic computerised space. It is encompassed by the Internet such as the World Wide Web (www). In simple words, it is the electronic digital world for communicating or accessing information over computer networks without physical movement of the sender and the receiver... It is also referred to as the Internet. There were less than 50 million Internet users in 1995, about 400 million in 2000 A.D. and over two billion in 2010. Now the majority of the world's users are in U.S.A., U.K., Germany, Japan, China and India.

Exercise

1. The Trans–Continental Stuart Highway runs between –
   (a) Darwin and Melbourne
   (b) Edmonton and Anchorage
   (c) Vancouver and St. John's City
   (d) Chengdu and Lhasa

2. Which country has the highest density of railway network?
   (a) Brazil
   (b) U.S.A
   (c) Canada
   (d) Russia

3. The Big Trunk Route runs through -
   (a) The Mediterranean – Indian ocean
   (b) The North Atlantic Ocean
   (c) The South Atlantic Ocean
   (d) The North Pacific Ocean

4. The Big Inch pipeline transports -
   (a) Milk
   (b) Liquid petroleum gas (LPG)
   (c) Water
   (d) Petroleum

5. Which one pair of the following places is linked by Channel Tunnel?
   (a) London – Berlin
   (b) Paris – London
   (c) Berlin – Paris
   (d) Barcelona – Berlin

6. Which of the following mode of transportation do not carry passengers and freight?
   (a) Pipelines
   (b) Air
   (c) Water
   (d) Land

7. The first public railway line was opened in ________ between Stockton and Darlington in northern England and then onwards, railways became the most popular and fastest form of transport in the nineteenth century.
   (a) 1820
   (b) 1825
   (c) 1830
   (d) 1835

8. Which of the following national highway connects Varanasi with Kanya Kumari?
   (a) NH 5
   (b) NH 6
   (c) NH 7
   (d) NH 8

9. Roads laid along ______________ boundaries are called border roads.
   (a) National
   (b) State
   (c) Inter-state
   (d) International

10. The Orient Express line runs through –
    (a) Paris to Istanbul
    (b) Paris to London
    (c) Paris to Egypt
    (d) Paris to Iceland

11. Communication through satellites emerged as a new area in communication technology since the ______ after U.S.A. and former U.S.S.R. pioneered space research.
    (a) 1950s
    (b) 1960s
    (c) 1970s
    (d) 1980s

12. Aryabhatt satellite was launched in which of the following year?
    (a) 1975
    (b) 1979
    (c) 1980
    (d) 1989

13. The Suez Canal had been constructed in ______ in Egypt between Port Said in the north and Port Suez in the south linking the Mediterranean Sea and the Red Sea.
    (a) 1869
    (b) 1870
    (c) 1879
    (d) 1889

14. Which canal connects the Atlantic Ocean in the east to the Pacific Ocean in the west?
    (a) Suez
    (b) Panama
    (c) Both
    (d) None

15. Volga river drains into which of the following sea?
    (a) Caspian sea
    (b) Mediterranean sea
    (c) Black sea
    (d) Red sea

16. The development of waterways depends on which of the following factors?
    1. Navigability
    2. width and depth of the channel
    3. continuity in the water flow
    4. transport technology in use
    Select the correct answer using the code given below:
    (a) 1 and 3 only
    (b) 2 and 4 only
    (c) 1, 2 and 3 only
    (d) 1, 2, 3 and 4

17. Consider the following statements:
    1. Compared to land and air, ocean transport is costly means of haulage (carrying of load) of bulky material over long distances from one continent to another.
    2. Modern passenger liners (ships) and cargo ships are equipped with radar, wireless and other navigation aids.

3. The development of refrigerated chambers for perishable goods, tankers and specialised ships has also improved cargo transport.

Which of the statements given above are correct?

(a) 1 and 2 only

(b) 1 and 3 only

(c) 2 and 3 only

(d) 1, 2 and 3

18. **Assertion:** One of the great advantages of water transportation is that it does not require route construction.

   Reasoning: The oceans are linked with each other and are negotiable with ships of various sizes.

   (a) Both the Assertion and the Reason are correct and the Reason is the correct explanation of the Assertion.

   (b) Both the Assertion and the Reason are correct but the Reason is not the correct explanation of the Assertion.

   (c) The Assertion is incorrect but the Reason is correct.

   (d) The Assertion is correct but the Reason is incorrect.

19. Consider the following statements:

   1. The world's total motorable road length is only about 15 million km, of which North America accounts for 33 per cent.

   2. The highest road density and the highest number of vehicles are registered in this continent compared to Western Europe.

   Which of the statements given above is/are correct?

   (a) 1 only

   b) 2 only

   (c) Both 1 and 2

   (d) Neither 1 nor 2

20. Which of the following are modes of transportation?

   1. Land   2. Water

   3. Air   4. Pipeline

   Select the correct answer using the code given below:

   (a) 1 and 3 only

   (b) 2 and 4 only

   (c) 1, 2 and 3 only

   (d) 1, 2, 3 and 4

Answers

1. (a) **2.** (b) **3.** (b) **4.** (d) **5.** (b) **6.** (a) **7.** (b) **8.** (c) **9.** (d) **10.** (a)

11. (c) **12.** (b) **13.** (a) **14.** (b) **15.** (a) **16.** (d) **17.** (c) **18.** (a) **19.** (c) **20.** (d)

CHAPTER 9

International Trade

❖ Trade may be conducted at two levels: international and national. International trade is the exchange of goods and services among countries across national boundaries.

❖ The initial form of trade in primitive societies was the barter system, where direct exchange of goods took place. The difficulties of barter system were overcome by the introduction of money. In the olden times, before paper and coin currency came into being, rare objects with very high intrinsic value served as money, like, flintstones, obsidian, *cowrie* shells, tiger's paws, whale's teeth, dogs teeth, skins, furs, cattle, rice, peppercorns, salt, small tools, copper, silver and gold.

❖ History of International Trade - In ancient times, transporting goods over long distances was risky, hence trade was restricted to local markets. The Silk Route is an early example of long distance trade connecting Rome to China – along the 6,000 km route. The traders transported Chinese silk, Roman wool and precious metals and many other high value commodities from intermediate points in India, Persia and Central Asia. After the disintegration of the Roman Empire, European commerce grew during twelfth and thirteenth century with the development of ocean going warships trade between Europe and Asia grew and the Americas were discovered. Fifteenth century onwards, the European colonialism began and along with trade of exotic commodities, a new form of trade emerged which was called slave trade. The Portuguese, Dutch, Spaniards, and British captured African natives and forcefully transported them to the newly discovered Americas for their labour in the plantations. Slave trade was a lucrative business for more than two hundred years till it was abolished in Denmark in 1792, Great Britain in 1807 and United States in 1808. After the Industrial Revolution the demand for raw materials like grains, meat, wool also expanded, but their monetary value declined in relation to the manufactured goods. During the World Wars I and II, countries imposed trade taxes and quantitative restrictions for the first time. During the postwar period, organisations like General Agreement for Tariffs and Trade (which later became the World Trade Organisation), helped in reducing tariff.

❖ International trade is based on the principle of comparative advantage, complimentarity and transferability of goods and services and in principle, should be mutually beneficial to the trading partners.

❖ Basis of International Trade -

(i) *Difference in national resources:* The world's national resources are unevenly distributed because of differences in their physical make up i.e. geology, relief soil and climate.

  (a) *Geological structure:* It determines the mineral resource base and topographical differences ensure diversity of crops and animals raised. Lowlands have greater agricultural potential. Mountains attract tourists and promote tourism.

  (b) *Mineral resources:* They are unevenly distributed the world over. The availability of mineral resources provides the basis for industrial development.

  (c) *Climate:* It influences the type of flora and fauna that can survive in a given region. It also ensures diversity in the range of various products, e.g. wool production can take place in cold regions, bananas, rubber and cocoa can grow in tropical regions.

(ii) *Population factors:* The size, distribution and diversity of people between countries affect the type and volume of goods traded.

  (a) *Cultural factors:* Distinctive forms of art and craft develop in certain cultures which are valued the world over, e.g. China produces the finest porcelains and brocades. Carpets of Iran are famous while North African leather work and Indonesian batik cloth are prized handicrafts.

(b) *Size of population:* Densely populated countries have large volume of internal trade but little external trade because most of the agricultural and industrial production is consumed in the local markets. Standard of living of the population determines the demand for better quality imported products because with low standard of living only a few people can afford to buy costly imported goods.

(iii) *Stage of economic development:* At different stages of economic development of countries, the nature of items traded undergo changes. In agriculturally important countries, agro products are exchanged for manufactured goods whereas industrialised nations export machinery and finished products and import food grains and other raw materials.

(iv) *Extent of foreign investment:* Foreign investment can boost trade in developing countries which lack in capital required for the development of mining, oil drilling, heavy engineering, lumbering and plantation agriculture. By developing such capital intensive industries in developing countries, the industrial nations ensure import of food stuffs, minerals and create markets for their finished products. This entire cycle steps up the volume of trade between nations.

(v) *Transport:* In olden times, lack of adequate and efficient means of transport restricted trade to local areas. Only high value items, e.g. gems, silk and spices were traded over long distances. With expansions of rail, ocean and air transport, better means of refrigeration and preservation, trade has experienced spatial expansion.

❖ Important Aspects of International Trade - International trade has three very important aspects. These are volume, sectoral composition and direction of trade.

❖ *Volume of Trade:* The actual tonnage of goods traded makes up the volume. However, services traded cannot be measured in tonnage. Therefore, the total value of goods and services traded is considered to be the volume of trade.

❖ *Composition of Trade:* Trade of primary products was dominant in the beginning of the last century. Later manufactured goods gained prominence and currently, though the manufacturing sector commands the bulk of the global trade, service sector which includes travel, transportation and other commercial services have been showing an upward trend. Fuels and mining goods and agricultural goods are also important contributors of merchandise exports.

❖ *Direction of Trade:* Historically, the developing countries of the present used to export valuable goods and artefacts, etc., which were exported to European countries. During the nineteenth century there was a reversal in the direction of trade. European countries started exporting manufactured goods for exchange of foodstuffs and raw materials from their colonies. Europe and U.S.A. emerged as major trade partners in the world and were leaders in the trade of manufactured goods. Japan at that time was also the third important trading country. The world trade pattern underwent a drastic change during the second half of the twentieth century. Europe lost its colonies while India, China and other developing countries started competing with developed countries. The nature of the goods traded has also changed.

❖ Balance of Trade - Balance of trade records the volume of goods and services imported as well as exported by a country to other countries. If the value of imports is more than the value of a country's exports, the country has negative or unfavourable balance of trade. If the value of exports is more than the value of imports, then the country has a positive or favourable balance of trade. Balance of trade and balance of payments have serious implications for a country's economy. A negative balance would mean that the country spends more on buying goods than it can earn by selling its goods. This would ultimately lead to exhaustion of its financial reserves.

❖ Types of International Trade - International trade may be categorised into two types:

(a) Bilateral trade: Bilateral trade is done by two countries with each other. They enter into agreement to trade specified commodities amongst them. For example, country A may agree to trade some raw material with agreement to purchase some other specified item to country B or vice versa.

(b) Multi-lateral trade: As the term suggests multi-lateral trade is conducted with many trading countries. The same country can trade with a number of other countries. The country may also grant the status of the "Most Favoured Nation" (MFN) on some of the trading partners.

❖ Case for Free Trade - The act of opening up economies for trading is known as free trade or trade liberalisation. This is done by bringing down trade barriers like tariffs. Trade liberalisation allows goods and services from everywhere to compete with domestic products and services. Globalisation along with free trade can adversely affect the economies of developing countries by not giving equal playing field by imposing conditions which are unfavourable. With the development of transport and communication systems goods and services can travel faster and farther than ever before. But free trade should not only let rich countries enter the markets, but allow the developed countries to keep their own markets protected from foreign products. Countries also need to be cautious about dumped goods; as along with free trade dumped goods of cheaper prices can harm the domestic producers.

❖ World Trade Organisation – In 1948, to liberalise the world from high customs tariffs and various other types of restrictions, General Agreement for Tariffs and Trade (GATT) was formed by some countries. In 1994, it was decided by the member countries to set up a permanent institution for looking after the promotion of free and fair trade amongst nation and the GATT was transformed into the World Trade Organisation from 1ˢᵗ January 1995. WTO is the only international organization dealing with the global rules of trade between nations. It sets the rules for the global trading system and resolves disputes between its member nations. WTO also covers trade in services, such as telecommunication and banking, and others issues such as intellectual rights.

❖ Regional Trade Blocs - Regional Trade Blocs have come up in order to encourage trade between countries with geographical proximity, similarity and complementarities in trading items and to curb restrictions on trade of the developing world. Today, 120 regional trade blocs generate 52 per cent of the world trade. These trading blocs developed as a response to the failure of the global organisations to speed up intra-regional trade. Though, these regional blocs remove trade tariffs within the member nations and encourage free trade, in the future it could get increasingly difficult for free trade to take place between different trading blocs.

❖ Concerns Related to International Trade - Undertaking international trade is mutually beneficial to nations if it leads to regional specialisation, higher level of production, better standard of living, worldwide availability of goods and services, equalisation of prices and wages and diffusion of knowledge and culture. International trade can prove to be detrimental to nations of it leads to dependence on other countries, uneven levels of development, exploitation, and commercial rivalry leading to wars. As countries compete to trade more, production and the use of natural resources spiral up, resources get used up faster than they can be replenished. As a result, marine life is also depleting fast, forests are being cut down and river basins sold off to private drinking water companies. Multinational corporations trading in oil, gas mining, pharmaceuticals and agri-business keep expanding their operations at all costs creating more pollution – their mode of work does not follow the norms of sustainable development. If organisations are geared only towards profit making, and environmental and health concerns are not addressed, then it could lead to serious implications in the future.

❖ Ports - The chief gateways of the world of international trade are the harbours and ports. Cargoes and travellers pass from one part of the world to another through these ports. The ports provide facilities of docking, loading, unloading and the storage facilities for cargo. In order to provide these facilities, the port authorities make arrangements for maintaining navigable channels, arranging tugs and barges, and providing labour and managerial services. The importance of a port is judged by the size of cargo and the number of ships handled. The quantity of cargo handled by a port is an indicator of the level of development of its hinterland.

❖ Types of Port - Generally, ports are classified according to the types of traffic which they handle.

● Types of port according to cargo handled:

   (i) *Industrial Ports:* These ports specialise in bulk cargo-like grain, sugar, ore, oil, chemicals and similar materials.

   (ii) *Commercial Ports:* These ports handle general cargo-packaged products and manufactured goods. These ports also handle passenger traffic.

   (iii) *Comprehensive Ports:* Such ports handle bulk and general cargo in large volumes. Most of the world's great ports are classified as comprehensive ports.

● Types of port on the basis of location:

   (i) *Inland Ports:* These ports are located away from the sea coast. They are linked to the sea through a river or a canal. Such ports are accessible to flat bottom ships or barges. For example, Manchester is linked with a canal; Memphis is located on the river Mississippi; Rhine has several ports like Mannheim and Duisburg; and Kolkata is located on the river Hoogli, a branch of the river Ganga.

(ii) *Out Ports:* These are deep water ports built away from the actual ports. These serve the parent ports by receiving those ships which are unable to approach them due to their large size. Classic combination, for example, is Athens and its out port Piraeus in Greece.

- Types of port on the basis of specialized functions:

    (i) *Oil Ports:* These ports deal in the processing and shipping of oil. Some of these are tanker ports and some are refinery ports. Maracaibo in Venezuela, Esskhira in Tunisia, Tripoli in Lebanon are tanker ports. Abadan on the Gulf of Persia is a refinery port.

    (ii) *Ports of Call:* These are the ports which originally developed as calling points on main sea routes where ships used to anchor for refuelling, watering and taking food items. Later on, they developed into commercial ports. Aden, Honolulu and Singapore are good examples.

    (iii) *Packet Station:* These are also known as *ferry ports.* These packet stations are exclusively concerned with the transportation of passengers and mail across water bodies covering short distances. These stations occur in pairs located in such a way that they face each other across the water body, e.g. Dover in England and Calais in France across the English Channel.

    (iv) *Entrepot Ports:* These are collection centres where the goods are brought from different countries for export. Singapore is an entrepot for Asia. Rotterdam for Europe, and Copenhagen for the Baltic region.

    (v) *Naval Ports:* These are ports which have only strategic importance. These ports serve warships and have repair workshops for them. Kochi and Karwar are examples of such ports in India.

Exercise

1. Most of the world's great ports are classified as:
   - (a) Naval Ports
   - (b) Oil Ports
   - (c) Comprehensive Ports
   - (d) Industrial Ports

2. Which one of the following continents has the maximum flow of global trade?
   - (a) Asia
   - (b) North America
   - (c) Europe
   - (d) Africa

3. Which one of the following South American nation is a part of OPEC?
   - (a) Brazil
   - (b) Chile
   - (c) Venezuela
   - (d) Peru

4. In which of the following trade blocs, is India an associate member?
   - (a) SAFTA
   - (b) OECD
   - (c) ASEAN
   - (d) OPEC

5. The initial form of trade in primitive societies was the _______ system, where direct exchange of goods took place.
   - (a) Exchange
   - (b) Market
   - (c) Goods
   - (d) Barter

6. The _______ Route is an early example of long distance trade connecting Rome to China – along the 6,000 km route.
   - (a) Silk
   - (b) Diamond
   - (c) Wool
   - (d) Masala

7. The practice of selling a commodity in two countries at a price that differs for reasons not related to costs is called _______ .
   - (a) Selling
   - (b) Dumping
   - (c) Picking
   - (d) Buying

8. In which of the following year WTO formed?
   - (a) 1994
   - (b) 1995
   - (c) 1996
   - (d) 1997

9. CIS stands for –
   - (a) Common of Independent States
   - (b) Commonwealth of Independence States
   - (c) Commonwealth of Independent States
   - (d) Commonwealth of Independent Status

10. Latin American Integration Association was formed in which of the following year?
    - (a) 1991
    - (b) 1992
    - (c) 1993
    - (d) 1994

11. These are the ports which originally developed as calling points on main sea routes where ships used to anchor for refuelling, watering and taking food items. Later on, they developed into commercial ports.

    Above statements defines which of the following port?
    - (a) Inland Ports
    - (b) Ports of Call
    - (c) Industrial Ports
    - (d) Commercial Ports

12. These ports are located away from the sea coast. They are linked to the sea through a river or a canal. Such ports are accessible to flat bottom ships or barges.

    Above statements defines which of the following port?
    - (a) Inland Ports
    - (b) Out Ports
    - (c) Industrial Ports
    - (d) Commercial Ports

13. **Assertion:** The act of opening up economies for trading is known as free trade or trade liberalisation.

    Reasoning: This is done by bringing down trade barriers like tariffs.
    - (a) Both the Assertion and the Reason are correct and the Reason is the correct explanation of the Assertion.
    - (b) Both the Assertion and the Reason are correct but the Reason is not the correct explanation of the Assertion.
    - (c) The Assertion is incorrect but the Reason is correct.
    - (d) The Assertion is correct but the Reason is incorrect.

14. Which of the following is/are Types of International Trade?
    - (a) Bilateral trade
    - (b) Multi-lateral trade
    - (c) Both
    - (d) None

15. Which of the following is/are the important aspects of the International Trade?
    1. Volume of Trade
    2. Composition of Trade
    3. Direction of Trade

    Select the correct answer using the code given below:
    - (a) 2 only
    - (b) 3 only
    - (c) 1 and 2 only
    - (d) 1, 2 and 3

16. Which of the following are the Basis of International Trade?

1. Difference in national resources
2. Population factors
3. Stage of economic development
4. Extent of foreign investment
5. Transport

Select the correct answer using the code given below:

(a) 1, 3 and 5 only   (b) 2 and 4 only

(c) 2, 3, 4 and 5 only   (d) 1, 2, 3, 4 and 5

17. General Agreement for Tariffs and Trade later became –

(a) World Trade Organisation

(b) International Monetary Fund

(c) World Bank

(d) Free Trade Agreement

18. Consider the following statements:

1. Fifteenth century onwards, the European colonialism began and along with trade of exotic commodities, a new form of trade emerged which was called slave trade.
2. The Portuguese, Dutch, Spaniards, and British captured African natives and forcefully transported them to the newly discovered Americas for their labour in the plantations.
3. Slave trade was a lucrative business for more than two hundred years till it was abolished in Denmark in 1792, Great Britain in 1807 and United States in 1808.

Which of the statements given above is/are correct?

(a) 3 only   (b) 2 only

(c) 1 only   (d) 1, 2 and 3

19. In the olden times, before paper and coin currency came into being, rare objects with very high intrinsic value served as money. Which of the following were used as money?

1. flintstones   2. obsidian
3. cowrie shells   4. tiger's paws
5. whale's teeth

Select the correct answer using the code given below:

(a) 2 and 4 only   (b) 1, 3 and 5 only

(c) 1, 2, 3 and 4 only   (d) 1, 2, 3, 4 and 5

20. Consider the following statements:

1. Trade may be conducted at two levels: international and national.
2. National trade is the exchange of goods and services among countries across national boundaries.
3. Countries need to trade to obtain commodities, they cannot produce themselves or they can purchase elsewhere at a lower price.

Which of the statements given above is/are correct?

(a) 1 and 2 only

(b) 1 and 3 only

(c) 2 and 3 only

(d) 1, 2 and 3

Answers

1. (c)   **2.** (b)   **3.** (c)   **4.** (a)   **5.** (d)   **6.** (a)   **7.** (b)   **8.** (b)   **9.** (c)   **10.** (d)

11. (b)   **12.** (a)   **13.** (b)   **14.** (c)   **15.** (d)   **16.** (d)   **17.** (a)   **18.** (d)   **19.** (d)   **20.** (b)

CHAPTER 10

Human Settlement

Chapter at glance

Introduction

❖ The study of human settlements is basic to human geography because the form of settlement in any particular region reflects human relationship with the environment.

❖ A human settlement is defined as a place inhabited more or less permanently.

❖ The houses may be designed or redesigned, buildings may be altered, functions may change but settlement continues in time and space.

❖ There may be some settlements which are temporary and are occupied for short periods, may be a season.

Classification of Settlements Rural Urban Dichotomy

❖ Settlements can be differentiated in terms of rural and urban, but there is no consensus on what exactly defines a village or a town.

❖ Although population size is an important criterion, it is not a universal criterion since many villages in densely populated countries of India and China have population exceeding that of some towns of Western Europe and United States.

❖ At one time, people living in villages pursued agriculture or other primary activities, but presently in developed countries, large sections of urban populations prefer to live in villages even though they work in the city.

❖ The basic difference between towns and villages is that in towns the main occupation of the people is related to secondary and tertiary sectors, while in the villages most of the people are engaged in primary occupations such as agriculture, fishing, lumbering, mining, animal husbandry, etc.

Types and Patterns of Settlements

Settlements may also be classified by their shape, patterns types. The major types classified by shape are:

i. **Compact or Nucleated settlements:** These settlements are those in which large number of houses are built very close to each other. Such settlements develop along river valleys and in fertile plains. Communities are closely knit and share common occupations.

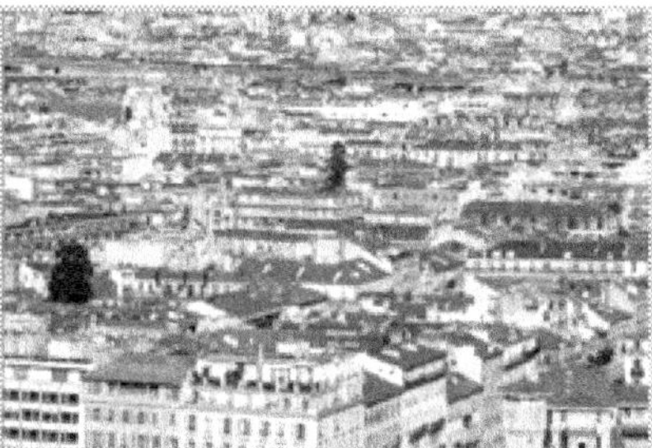

ii. Dispersed Settlements: In these settlements, houses are spaced far apart and often interspersed with fields. A cultural feature such as a place of worship or a market, binds the settlement together.

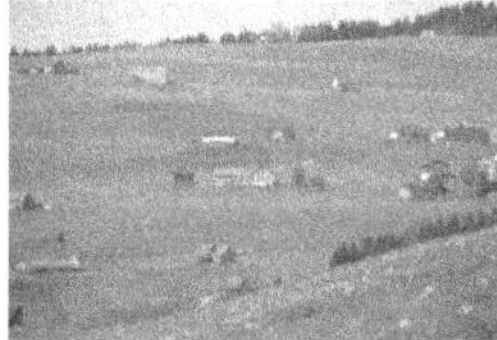

Rural Settlements

❖ Rural settlements are most closely and directly related to land. They are dominated by primary activities such as agriculture, animal husbandry, fishing etc. The settlements size is relatively small. Some factors affecting the location of rural settlements are :

i. **Water Supply**

- Usually rural settlements are located near water bodies such as rivers, lakes, and springs where water can be easily obtained.

- Sometimes the need for water drives people to settle in otherwise disadvantaged sites such as islands surrounded by swamps or low lying river banks.

- Most water based 'wet point' settlements have many advantages such as water fordrinking, cooking and washing. Rivers and lakes can be used to irrigate farm land.
- Water bodies also have fish which can be caught for diet and navigable rivers and lakes can be used for transportation.

ii. Land

- People choose to settle near fertile lands suitable for agriculture.
- In Europe villages grew up near rolling country avoiding swampy, low lying land while people in south east Asia chose to live near low lying river valleys and coastal plains suited for wet rice cultivation.
- Early settlers chose plain areas with fertile soils.

iii. Upland

- Upland which is not prone to flooding was chosen to prevent damage to houses and loss of life.
- Thus, in low lying river basins people chose to settle on terraces and levees which are "dry points".
- In tropical countries people build their houses on stilts near marshy lands to protect themselves from flood, insects and animal pests.

iv. Building Material

- The availability of building materials- wood, stone near settlements is another advantage. Early villages were built in forest clearings where wood was plentiful.

v. Defence

- During the times of political instability, war, hostility of neighbouring groups villages were built on defensive hills and islands.
- In Nigeria, upstanding inselbergs formed good defensive sites. In India most of the forts are located on higher grounds or hills.

vi. Planned Settlements

- Sites that are not spontaneously chosen by villagers themselves, planned settlements are constructed by governments by providing shelter, water and other infrastructures on acquired lands.
- The scheme of villagisation in Ethiopia and the canal colonies in Indira Gandhi canal command area in India are some good examples

Rural Settlement Patterns

❖ Patterns of rural settlements reflect the way the houses are sited in relation to each other. The site of the village, the surrounding topography and terrain influence the shape and size of a village. Rural settlements may be classified on the basis of a number of criteria:

i. **On the basis of setting:** The main types are plain villages, plateau villages, coastal villages, forest villages and desert villages

ii. **On the basis of functions:** There may be farming villages, fishermen's villages, lumberjack villages, pastoral villages etc.

iii. **On the basis of forms or shapes of the settlements:** These may be a number of geometrical forms and shapes such as Linear, rectangular, circular star like, T-shaped village, double village, cross-shaped village etc.

    a. **Linear pattern:** In such settlements houses are located along a road, railway line, river, canal edge of a valley or along a levee.

    b. **Rectangular pattern:** Such patterns of rural settlements are found in plain areas or wide inter montane valleys. The roads are rectangular and cut each other at right angles.

    c. **Circular pattern:** Circular villages develop around lakes, tanks and sometimes the village is planned in such a way that the central part remains open and is used for keeping the animals to protect them from wild animal.

    d. **Star like pattern:** Where several roads converge, star shaped settlements develop by the houses built along the roads.

    e. **T-shaped, Y-shaped, Cross-shaped or cruciform settlements:** T-shapedsettlements develop at tri-junctions of the roads while Y-shaped settlements emerge as the places where two roads converge on the third one and houses are built along these roads. Cruciform settlements develop on the cross-roads and houses extend in all the four direction.

    f. **Double village:** These settlements extend on both sides of a river where there is a bridge or a ferry.

Problems of Rural Settlements

❖ Rural settlements in the developing countries are large in number and poorly equipped with infrastructure.

❖ Supply of water to rural settlements in developing countries is not adequate.

❖ People in villages, particularly in mountainous and arid areas have to walk long distances to fetch drinking water.

❖ Water borne diseases such as cholera and jaundice tend to be a common problem.

❖ The general absence of toilet and garbage disposal facilities cause health related problems.

❖ The design and use of building materials of houses vary from one ecological region to another.

❖ The houses made up of mud, wood and thatch, remain susceptible to damage during heavy rains and floods, and require proper maintenance every year.

❖ Most house designs are typically deficient in proper ventilation. Besides, the design of a house includes the animal shed along with its fodderstore within it.

❖ This is purposely done to keep the domestic animals and their food properly protected from wild animals.

❖ Unmetalled roads and lack of modern communication network creates a unique problem.

❖ During rainy season, the settlements remain cut off and pose serious difficulties in providing emergency services.

❖ It is also difficult to provide adequate health and educational infrastructure for their large rural population.

❖ The problem is particularly serious where proper villagisation has not taken place and houses are scattered over a large area.

Urban Settlement

❖ Rapid urban growth is a recent phenomenon.

Classification

❖ Some of the common basis of classification are size of population, occupational structure and administrative setup.

❖ **Population Size:** It is an important criteria used by most countries to define urban areas.

- Besides the size of population, density of 400 persons per sq km and share of non-agricultural workers are taken into consideration in India.

❖ **Occupational Structure:** In some countries, such as India, the major economic activities in addition to the size of the population in designating a settlement as urban are also taken as a criterion.

- Similarly, in Italy, a settlement is called urban, if more than 50 per cent of its economically productive population is engaged in non-agricultural pursuits. India has set this criterion at 75 per cent.

❖ **Administration:** The administrative setup is a criterion for classifying a settlement as urban in some countries.

- For example, in India, a settlement of any size is classified as urban, if it has a municipality, Cantonment Board or Notified Area Council.

- Similarly, in Latin American countries, such as Brazil and Bolivia, any administrative centre is considered urban irrespective of its population size.

❖ **Location:** Location of urban centres is examined with reference to their function.

- Strategic towns require sites offering natural defence; mining towns require the presence of economically valuable minerals; industrial towns generally need local energy supplies or raw materials; tourist centres require attractive scenery, or a marine beach, a spring with medicinal water or historical relics, ports require a harbouretc

- Locations of the earliest urban settlements were based on the availability of water, building materials and fertile land.

- Apart from site, the situation plays an important role in the expansion of towns.

❖ **Functions of Urban Centres:** The earliest towns were centres of administration, trade, industry, defence and religious importance.

- The significance of defence and religion as differentiating functions has declined in general, but other functions have entered the list.

- In spite of towns performing multiple functions we refer to their dominant function.

- Most of the early nineteenth-century fishing ports in England have now developed tourism.

- Many of the old market towns are now known for manufacturing activities.

- Towns and cities are classified into the following categories.

❖ **Administrative Towns:** National capitals, which house the administrative offices of central governments, such as New Delhi, Canberra, Beijing, Addis Ababa, Washington D.C., and London etc. are called administrative towns.

- Provincial (sub-national) towns can also have administrative functions, for example, Victoria (British Columbia), Albany (New York), Chennai (Tamil Nadu).

❖ **Trading and Commercial Towns:** Agricultural market towns, such as, Winnipeg and Kansas city; banking and financial centres like Frankfurt and Amsterdam; large inland centres like Manchester and St Louis; and transport nodes such as, Lahore, Baghdad and Agra have been important trading centres.

❖ **Cultural Towns:** Places of pilgrimage, such as Jerusalem, Mecca, JagannathPuri and Varanasi etc. are considered cultural towns. These urban centres are of great religious importance.

- Additional functions which the cities perform are health and recreation (Miami and Panaji), industrial (Pittsburgh and Jamshedpur), mining and quarrying (Broken Hill and Dhanbad) and transport (Singapore and Mughal Sarai).

Classification of Towns On The Basis Of Forms

The form of the settlement, architecture and style of buildings and other structures are an outcome of its historical and cultural traditions.

❖ Towns and cities of developed and developing countries reflect marked differences in planning and development.

❖ While most cities in developed countries are planned, most urban settlements of developing countries have evolved historically with irregular shapes.

❖ For example, Chandigarh and Canberra are planned cities, while smaller town in India have evolved historically from walled cities to large urban sprawls.

❖ **Addis Ababa (The New Flower):** The name of Ethiopian capital Addis Ababa, as the name indicates (Addis-New, Ababa-Flower) is a 'new' city which was established in 1878.

- The whole city is located on a hill-valley topography.

- The roads radiate from the govt headquarters Piazza, Arat and Amist Kilo roundabouts. Mercato has markets which grew with time and is supposed to be the largest market between Cairo and Johannesburg.

❖ Canberra: Canberra was planned as the capital of Australia in 1912 by American landscape architect, Walter Burley Griffin.

- He had envisaged a garden city for about 25,000 people taking into account the natural features of the landscape. There were to be five main centreseach with separate city functions.

Types of Urban Settlements

❖ **Towns:** The concept of 'town' can best be understood with reference to 'village'. Population size is not the only criterion.

- Functional contrasts between towns and villages may not always be clearcut, but specific functions such as, manufacturing, retail and wholesale trade, and professional services exist in towns.

❖ **City:** A city may be regarded as a leading town, which has outstripped its local or regional rivals. In the words of Lewis Mumford, " the city is in fact the physical form of the highest and most complex type of associative life".

- Cities are much larger than towns and have a greater number of economic functions.

- They tend to have transport terminals, major financial institutions and regional administrative offices.

- When the population crosses the one million mark it is designated as a million city.

❖ **Conurbation:** The term conurbation was coined by Patrick Geddes in 1915 and applied to a large area of urban development that resulted from the merging of originally separate towns or cities.

- Greater London, Manchester, Chicago and Tokyo are examples.

❖ **Megalopolis:** This Greek word meaning "great city", was popularised by Jean Gottman (1957) and signifies 'super- metropolitan' region extending,as union of conurbations.

- The urban landsca pe stretching from Boston in the north to south of Washington in U.S.A. is the best known example of a megalopolis.

❖ **Million City:** The number of million cities in the world has been increasing as never before.The rate of increase in the number of million cities has been three-fold in every three decades.

❖ **Distribution of Mega Cities:**A mega city or megalopolis is a general term for cities together with their suburbs with a population of more than 10 million people.

- The number of mega cities has increased in the developing countries during the last 50 years vis-à-vis the developed countries.

Problems of Human Settlements in Developing Countries

- ❖ The settlements in developing countries, suffer from various problems, such as unsustainable concentration of population, congested housing and streets, lack of drinking water facilities.
- ❖ They also lack infrastructure such as, electricity, sewage disposal, health and education facilities.

Problems of Urban Settlements

- ❖ Shortage of housing, vertical expansion and growth of slums are characteristic features of modern cities of developing countries
- ❖ In many cities an increasing proportion of the population lives in substandard housing, e.g. slums and squatter settlements.
- ❖ In most million plus cities in India, one in four inhabitants lives in illegal settlements, which are growing twice as fast as the rest of the cities.
- ❖ **Economic Problems:** The decreasing employment opportunities in the rural as well as smaller urban areas of the developing countries consistently push the population to the urban areas.
- ❖ **Socio-cultural Problems:** Cities in the developing countries suffer from several social ills. Insufficient financial resources fail to create adequate social infrastructure catering to the basic needs of the huge population.
  - The available educational and health facilities remain beyond the reach of the urban poor.
  - Health indices also, present a gloomy picture in cities of developing countries.
  - Lack of employment and education tends to aggravate the crime rates. Male selective migration to the urban areas distorts the sex ratio in these cities.
- ❖ **Environmental Problems:** The large urban population in developing countries not only uses but also disposes off a huge quantity of water and all types of waste materials.
  - Many cities of the developing countries even find it extremely difficult to provide the minimum required quantity of potable water and water for domestic and industrial uses.
  - Massive use of traditional fuel in the domestic as well as the industrial sector severely pollutes the air.
  - The domestic and industrial wastes are either let into the general sewerages or dumped without treatment at unspecified locations.
  - Huge concrete structures erected to accommodate the population and economic play a very conducive role to create heat islands.

Exercise

1. Which of the following statements are true about human settlements?

   I. Settlements can be rural and urban.

   II. Population size is universal criterion.

   (a) I only (b) II only

   (c) Both I and II (d) Neither I nor II

2. Which of the following activities are primary in nature?

   I. Lumbering II. Fishing

   III. Mining IV. Rearing

   (a) I, II and III (b) II and IV

   (c) I, II and IV (d) All of the above

3. Which one of the following types of economic activities dominates in all rural settlement?

   (a) Primary (b) Secondary

   (c) Tertiary (d) Quaternary

4. Settlement that develops near the river valleys and fertile plains is known as –

   (a) Dispersed settlement

   (b) Compact settlement

   (c) Sub-urbanised settlement

   (d) Rural settlement

5. Cultural feature of a settlement where a settlement is bind together through market or place of worship is –

   (a) Urban settlement

   (b) Rural settlement

   (c) Nucleated settlement

   (d) Dispersed settlement

6. Usually rural settlements are located near water bodies such as rivers, lakes, and springs due to the following reason:

   (a) Water can be easily obtained

   (b) Lack of supplied water

   (c) To keep the water bodies cleaned

   (d) All of the above

7. People in South East Asia chose to live near low lying river valleys and coastal plains as –

   (a) Urban areas are over populated

   (b) It is suitable for wet rice cultivation

   (c) It promotes tourism

   (d) It is useful for trade with other countries

8. Which of the following pairs are incorrect?

   (a) Loess : China

   (b) Savannas : Africa

   (c) Eskimos : Polar region

   (d) Igloo : Greenland

9. Which of the following statements are correct about planned settlements?

   I. Sites are chosen spontaneously by the villagers.

   II. Government provides shelter, water and other infrastructures on the acquired land.

   III. Indira Gandhi canal command area is an example of it.

   (a) I only (b) II and III

   (c) I and II (d) All of the above

10. Assertion: Upland which is not prone to flooding was chosen to prevent damage to houses and loss of life.

    Reason: In tropical countries people build their houses on stilts near marshy lands to protect themselves from flood, insects and animal pests.

    (a) Both A and R are true and R is the correct explanation of A.

    (b) Both A and R are true and R is not the correct explanation of A.

    (c) A is true and R is false

    (d) A is false and R is true

11. Houses located along a levee is which type of pattern of settlement?

    (a) Rectangular (b) Upland

    (c) Linear (d) T shaped

12. Settlements found in the inter montane valleys are known as –

    (a) Linear (b) Circular

    (c) Y shaped (d) Rectangular

13. Which of the following are the problems in rural settlements?

    I. Inadequacy of water

    II. Absence of toilet

    III. Lack of modern communication

    (a) I and II

    (b) II and III

    (c) I and III

    (d) All of the above

14. Cholera and jaundice tend to be a common problem in the villages. These diseases are –

(a) Viral infection   (b) Water borne

(c) Bacterial infection   (d) Communicable

15. Which of the following countries are having population size of 250 person in urban area?

I. Denmark   II. Sweden

III. Finland   IV. Iceland

(a) I, II and III   (b) II, III and IV

(c) I, III and IV   (d) All of the above

16. In India, a settlement of any size is classified as urban if it is having –

(a) Transnational companies

(b) Public sector undertaking

(c) Municipality

(d) Solid waste management

17. Which of the following pair of settlement pattern is incorrectly matched with its feature?

(a) Star like pattern : develop by the houses built along the roads

(b) Circular pattern : village developed around lakes or any water body

(c) T- Shaped : settlements developed at the tri-junction of roads

(d) Cruciform : houses are located along a road and railway

18. Greater London, Manchester, Chicago and Tokyo are examples of –

(a) Administrative towns (b) Conurbans

(c) Rural settlements   (d) Trading centres

19. Which of the following are socio-cultural problems of urban settlements?

I. Insufficient financial resources to fulfill basic needs of the population

II. Sex ratio gets distorted due to infanticide

III. Urban poor could not afford available health and education facility

(a) I and II

(b) II and III

(c) I and III

(d) All of the above

20. Which of the following are parts of Urban Strategy laid down by United Nation Develop Programme?

I. Increasing shelter for rural and urban poor

II. Provision of Education, Primary Health care, Clean Water and Sanitation

III. Improving women's access to 'Basic Services' and government facilities

(a) I and II

(b) II and III

(c) I and III

(d) All of the above

Answers

1. (a)	**2.** (d)	**3.** (a)	**4.** (b)	**5.** (d)	**6.** (a)	**7.** (b)	**8.** (c)	**9.** (b)	**10.** (b)
11. (c)	**12.** (d)	**13.** (d)	**14.** (b)	**15.** (a)	**16.** (c)	**17.** (d)	**18.** (b)	**19.** (c)	**20.** (b)

Your Notes :

www.ingramcontent.com/pod-product-compliance
Lightning Source LLC
LaVergne TN
LVHW080619200726
843509LV00007B/345